The Growth Challenge

How To Build Your Business Profitably

Stephen A. Stumpf

Enterprise · Dearborn
a division of Dearborn Publishing Group, Inc.

While a great deal of care has been taken to provide accurate and current information, the ideas, suggestions, general principles and conclusions presented in this text are subject to local, state and federal laws and regulations, court cases and any revisions of same. The reader is thus urged to consult legal counsel regarding any points of law—this publication should not be used as a substitute for competent legal advice.

Publisher: Kathleen A. Welton
Acquisitions Editor: Patrick J. Hogan
Associate Editor: Karen A. Christensen
Senior Project Editor: Jack L. Kiburz
Interior Design: Lucy Jenkins
Cover Design: Lucy Jenkins

Printed in the United States of America

93 94 95 10 9 8 7 6 5 4 3 2 1

Library of Congress Cataloging-in-Publication Data

Stumpf, Stephen A.
   The growth challenge : how to build your business profitably /
Stephen A. Stumpf.
     p. cm.
   Includes index.
   ISBN 0-79310-468-8
   1. Small business—Growth.   I. Title.
HD62.7.S89   1993
658.02′2—dc20   92-47264
                                                                             CIP

DEDICATION

To Eugene S. Stumpf, who has been a new venture in our family since September 14, 1980. May his initiatives continue to bring us joy throughout our lives.

Contents

Preface

■————————————————————■

The biggest burden a growing company faces is having a full-blooded entrepreneur as its owner.

—Derek du Toit

If you insist on hiring executives below you in stature, you will soon find yourself running a pygmy business.

—David Ogilvy

Why, after successful start-ups, are many leaders of new ventures unclear about the direction of their business, unable to sustain and build support from their customers and employees or ill-prepared for the challenges of rapid growth? Why do so many small businesses stay small? Why is the United States losing its dominant global position in industries that it founded?

The Growth Challenge explores these questions through research and the experiences of new ventures that are in a period of rapid growth. Current advice encourages the leaders of businesses that have survived start-up to move away from being run by entrepreneurs—to hire professional managers and become professionally managed. *Transitioning from an entrepreneurial firm to a professionally managed firm prior to sustaining rapid growth for several years is premature advice.* It stifles growth (and profits) for the sake of control.

It is not until rapid growth slows and supply catches up with demand that the involvement, costs and temperament of professional managers is a viable alternative. What is needed during the rapid growth period are ways to sustain the growth rate while gradually increasing profits and cash flow. This requires the active leadership of people who can envision a future that includes their enterprise as a powerful competitor; it also requires people who can influence and inspire others to envision the goal and take actions to reach it. Such people must think, analyze and reflect on their business profit-loss dynamics, its direction and profitable growth. Then they must act. *The Growth Challenge* is about learning how to actively scan the environment so as to become quick, flexible and effective in every situation—from formulating ideas to influencing others.

Some say that during rapid growth the key challenge is financing—without it continued rapid growth is not possible. While financial resources are needed for rapid growth to continue, obtaining resources is rarely the new venture's key challenge. Because of the venture's rapid growth, additional financing is easier to obtain than during the venture's start-up period. Firms that obtain incremental financing easily are no more likely to sustain rapid growth than those that struggle to obtain such financing. Obtaining additional financing is not the key challenge; *the key challenge is understanding changes in a business as it grows and learning how to lead the venture effectively.*

The key challenge is leadership, not money. Dynamic models that stimulate ongoing discovery and learning in a rapidly changing environment are needed to develop that leadership. Skills of "professional managers" are not needed during the rapid growth period.

New venture managers must be leaders of people for their ventures to grow, not simply managers of activities and their own energy—whether they are entrepreneurs, small business owners or new product managers employed by corporations. The term *new venture manager* as used in *The Growth Challenge* is inclusive of entrepreneurs, small business owners, managers of small businesses and product managers within larger organizations. I chose the term *new venture manager* rather than *new venture leader* to distinguish what tends to exist from what is needed. Most people in charge of a newer business defined their role to me as a manager. As one person put it, "Everyone here claims to be a leader, and I am their manager."

The Growth Challenge is written for these new venture managers who have survived start-up and are now challenged with obtaining and sustaining rapid growth. While their business situations are surely different, many of their growth challenges are the same. They each must

• learn to lead others as well as their business;

- continually scan the environment for meaningful changes and opportunities (i.e., remain open to ideas);
- deny more and more of those opportunities to maintain focus;
- become quick, flexible and effective in all of their actions;
- find additional sources of capital;
- share control of the business with others;
- cope with confusion and employee resentment over ambiguous roles and responsibilities as business activity increases;
- accept the reality that they do not have the time, energy or capacity to run all aspects of the business by themselves; and
- develop new ways of thinking about their business that reflect its growth rate and size.

The Growth Challenge addresses these challenges by providing ways for new venture managers to gain clarity about the direction of their business, build support from their customers and employees and use several practical models and tools to obtain and sustain rapid growth.

Acknowledgments

The ideas and insights that I share have emerged over time from my involvement with dozens of people running small businesses or new ventures that were struggling with the challenges of creating and sustaining rapid growth. The entrepreneurs and new venture managers interviewed in this study, as well as the writings of others, have contributed greatly to my understanding of the challenges faced by new venture managers as they seek rapid growth. Sometimes the ideas shared in *The Growth Challenge* are rooted in an event I experienced; other times they have crystallized from vicarious experiences such as watching entrepreneurs, listening to them and asking questions.

I have chosen not to identify the entrepreneurs and new venture managers by name or company to respect their privacy. There is no "one best way" to grow a new venture rapidly and profitably. By discussing the situation and not disclosing the people or their ventures, I believe greater learning is likely on the part of others. Growing a business profitably is not a "copy what they did" activity. To grow a business rapidly and profitably, one must reflect on their business activities every day with a bias for action as new ideas emerge. Reflect, then act.

Some professionals, managers and entrepreneurs have written about their experiences in ways that have contributed to my understanding of the rapid growth period in a new venture—these I want to acknowledge specifically. Those who have influenced my thinking the most are Dale Zand, author of *Information, Organization, and Power: Effective Management in the Knowledge Society;* Paul Hawken, author of *Growing a Business* and founder of Smith & Hawken; and Thomas Mullen, coauthor of *Taking Charge: Strategic Leadership in the Middle Game.* I am indebted to each of these authors for their contributions to the field of business and to my forever-evolving understanding of it.

There are many others who have influenced me and my writings—a special thanks to Maria Arnone, Zenas Block, Joel DeLuca and Robert Longman as well as the new venture managers who participated in research that contributed to this book. Maria has been a partner in several new ventures—always there with enthusiasm and a willingness to take it the next step. Zenas is the wise visionary on the mount—guiding others to do what they previously only dreamed about. Joel is a philosopher-king—challenging my thinking on many topics at a moment's notice. To have a friend and colleague that provides such a rich stimulus is truly a blessing. Robert is the genius behind many of the models shared here; his ideas often helped me to understand the entrepreneurs' ideas.

Others have influenced me through our interactions and business activities: Sabra Brock, Andy Fleming, William Guth, Pam Horowitz, Suresh Kotha, Laura Landy, Candace Ulrich, Karen Watson and Trish Williams. These clients and colleagues have both stimulated new thoughts and provided forums in which ideas get put into action. I am indebted to them for their trust and support.

Many others have contributed indirectly to this book as part of a team, known as the Management Simulation Projects Group at New York University, and as affiliates of the MSP Institute, Inc.: Catherine Ahern, Deborah Barrows, Hrach Bedrosian, Roger Dunbar, Richard Green, Susan Heinbuch, Mary McBride, Sidney Nachman and Monica Shay.

No book ever makes it to press without the support of the publisher and its editorial staff. Patrick Hogan saw in the proposal for this book the opportunity for me and Dearborn Financial Publishing to make a meaningful contribution to entrepreneurship and leadership in America. Through his guidance and editorial assistance, we hope to have made that contribution real. My literary agent, Michael Snell, also contributed to this process, as did an anonymous reviewer.

I thank you all.

I greatly appreciate the neverending comfort provided by my family and friends who encourage me and support my research and writing endeavors. They have made this book possible.

Introduction

"When I started this business I was sure it would become a $100,000,000 enterprise in five years. The independent software packages we obtained a license to sell made the other programs on the market look like kids' toys. But things progressed faster than we expected, and we did not change fast enough. We are still a success, but our growth is much slower than we planned." (President of a computer software distribution firm six years after start-up.)

"The product concept was great. People could order our traveler's checks from anywhere and have them presigned with their signature by computer if they had their signature and a password on file. The traveler's checks would be mailed to their home or office. No more going to a bank to get them, no more last minute rushing around before a trip. The product was discontinued within two years. We never had the right people running it." (Manager of new product development at a commercial bank.)

"Most new products fail." (Marketing manager, Levi Strauss and Company, after the failure of the Tailored Classics menswear line in 1982.)

In contrast to this Levi Strauss marketing manager's belief, most new products that are brought to market *survive* for two to three years. They may fizzle or have slow growth after that, but they survive start-up. The issues they face poststart-up—18 months after the launch of the product or service—differ substantially in nature and process from the prestart-up and start-up activities.

It is true that most new ideas never lead to new products and that new product ideas are brought to market slowly with high failure rates by large organizations. Most new ideas are never given a chance. Many that are given a chance are managed to death by "seasoned managers" rather than led by an inspired, experienced champion and entrepreneur.

Ironically, some new products brought to market outlast the involvement of their new product managers, entrepreneurs, founders or start-up organization. Osborne brought one of the first personal computers to market. The Osborne executive computer is long gone, but the personal computer business sells billions of dollars worth of equipment each year.

It is estimated that 80 percent of all new businesses are no longer in existence or under the control of their founders or champions by the end of their tenth year; 50 percent may actually be out of business before five years. Sustaining rapid growth is not easy. Yet, over 75 percent of the new ventures that attain high rates of growth in their third to sixth years survive to a profitable maturity. Venture size and survival go together: new ventures (including new products offered by existing enterprises) that can achieve high rates of growth support more employees sooner and survive longer.

My interest in the rapid growth of new ventures stems from the belief that more than 20 percent of the new businesses created each year that survive start-up can achieve rapid growth and prosper well into the future. In conducting the research for and writing this book, I have had a particular reader in mind. I see you as

- proven survivors who are on quests to master some parts of your lives;
- individuals who are oriented toward problem solving, intelligent and open to the ideas of others;
- seasoned business people for whom some of the challenges of rapid growth are not new;
- people with a bias for action and a healthy respect for reflection and analysis.

You probably devote a few hours each week to reading, and you want the time invested to yield meaningful results. For this to occur here, you will need to engage the ideas shared and respond to many questions that relate to your situation. *The Growth Challenge* identifies hundreds of questions that are continually answered by the most successful new venture managers. Many of these questions take only a few moments to answer; others require active reflection, analysis and possibly even experimentation. The questions are organized in "sets" for you to address as you read or when a business situation arises that stimulates your recollection of a topic previously covered. As with other "handbooks," *The Growth Challenge* is meant to be used and reused. Write in it, bend the pages and leave markers to guide you back to the sections that are most useful to your business situation.

Some of the ideas in *The Growth Challenge* may initially strike you as basic—great! *It was the most basic ideas that the successful new venture managers returned to most often.* While an idea may be basic, its application to your business is rarely easy. The rules of hitting in baseball are basic. Swing level, make solid contact with the ball and follow through. Hitting home runs in your business is as difficult as it is in baseball. Basics get you started; skill in application keeps the business going and growing.

Your business has survived. Now you want to take actions to obtain and sustain rapid growth. You have developed substantial skill at asking and responding to questions associated with the start-up of your venture. You need to repeat the process, but with an altered set of questions, to attain rapid growth. *The Growth Challenge* is organized into three parts to help you accomplish this goal.

Part I applies proven business ideas to the new venture's poststart-up situation to plan for rapid growth and profitability. It gets you thinking and analyzing "the right stuff."

Part II focuses on the strategic leadership practices necessary to create and sustain rapid growth and profits. Clear direction, identifying stakeholders and influencing others are the key elements of leadership needed.

Part III examines the new venture manager skills and the learning necessary to sustain growth and increase profits. Leadership techniques that have been successfully used in the new venture activities of larger organizations are applied to the rapid growth of smaller ventures.

The initial questions to consider to achieve and sustain rapid growth are the focus of Part I, "A New Beginning." By the end of Part I, you will have developed several plans for "how to get there from here." These plans are a useful starting point. They are not the end result that you seek.

Part II, "Building the Business," details what you need to consider in terms of business objectives and customers as you begin to enact your plans. Strategic leadership ideas are used to facilitate a shift from analysis to implementation. You must go beyond establishing direction to sharing the directions sought with others.

At the end of Part II, the stage is set. The players are identified, informed and well practiced. The play has been written and well learned. If the rapid growth challenge was to "put the same play on every night for the entire season," the book would end at this point.

You know that the challenges of rapid growth are not constant; customers want change, competitors keep trying new things to win away your best customers, employees leave, product demand changes or a supplier goes out of business. In short, your play must be a dynamic one, involving the audience, critics, play writer and concession staff.

Part III, "Thrust or Drift into the Next Decade?", focuses on what only a few other books on new venture growth have even considered, namely, the human side of your venture—*people*. How do I get my people capable and willing to handle the many challenges of rapid growth as they occur, without waiting for my approval? Time is more than money—it is life itself.

The ideas in Part III, compared to Part I, are new. They are less well understood by people in business because of their newness. For many, these ideas will involve a shift in the way they think about the growth of their ventures in the future. For some, this may feel a bit uncomfortable at times, or it may seem to be a more abstract approach than the earlier parts of the book. It probably is.

The ideas presented in Part III are those that the most successful new venture managers espoused the strongest. They may not have always used the exact words that I have chosen, but they found the ideas shared herein to be an accurate reflection of their ideas when they were "played back to them."

I have chosen to use some jargon in Part III to clearly link the ideas emerging in successful new ventures to the only source of considered thought available—scholarly writing. What sounds like jargon today may well become tomorrow's buzz words. I hope so.

Part One

———■————————————————————■———

A New Beginning

Y our business, like most others, will progress through various product life-cycle stages. The prestart-up and pioneering stage, which includes start-up and survival, is in the past. Many life-cycle stages are still to come: early growth, expansion and rapid growth (the next three to ten years or so); slow growth, stability and maturity; and finally, no growth and decline. (See Figure I.1.)

Your venture is somewhere in stage two, and you want it to grow and deliver profits for many years to come. You would like it to reach the spot on the growth curve that is sweetest—rapid growth, significant profits and positive cash flow. This "sweet spot" occurs before the rate of growth begins to decline, as indicated on the product life-cycle diagram by the circle. It is useful to reflect on where your venture has been in preparation for the decisions you will make to attain and sustain rapid growth.

IN THE BEGINNING

In the creation of a new venture, new venture managers are generally driven by their own ideas and the ideas of close associates. The business environment that they both experience and create involves many changes, much ambiguity and continual uncertainty. Time feels severely compressed. Events do not occur in predictable patterns. Informal communications dominate; counterintuitive decisions, structures and procedures are tolerated. There are only a few formal control mechanisms for running the business.

Figure I.1   Life-Cycle Model and the Sweet Spot

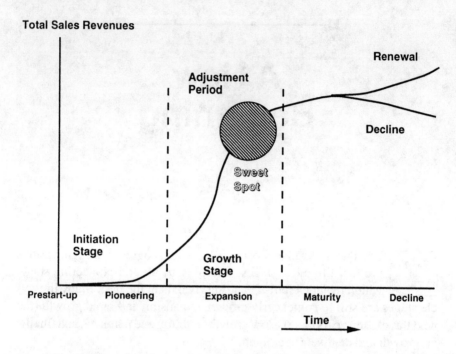

New venture managers develop much of their knowledge and experience in their endeavors as they go along—it is a learn-by-doing environment. The learning that takes place, as witnessed by a venture's survival, suggests that the new venture manager is one of the more (or most) knowledgeable people in the business.

WHERE YOU ARE NOW

As a venture begins to grow at high annual rates, the new venture manager's role shifts from doing things directly to influencing others to do things. The creativity the new venture manager brought to the business is eroded by the volume of activities associated with the business's success. Confusion and resentment among employees over ambiguous roles, responsibilities and goals may be occurring and becoming dysfunctional. The venture is not able to clone its founders and champions, and their energy is not sufficient to control and sustain the endeavor during rapid growth.

This rather undesirable and unpredicted environment raises serious questions. The most common questions new venture managers raised were

Figure I.2   The 4-Box Model—An Analytic Framework for Strategic Thinking

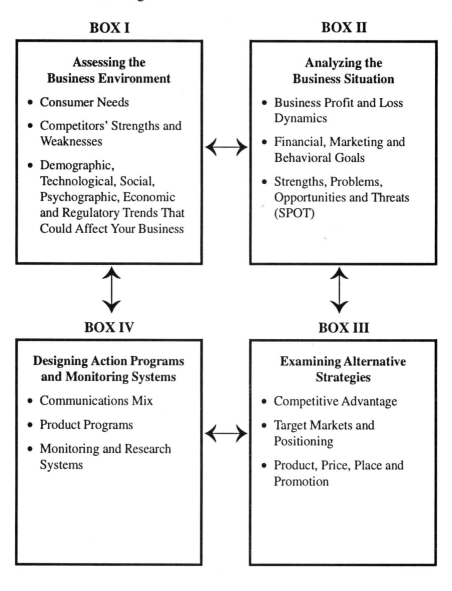

BOX I

Assessing the Business Environment

- Consumer Needs
- Competitors' Strengths and Weaknesses
- Demographic, Technological, Social, Psychographic, Economic and Regulatory Trends That Could Affect Your Business

BOX II

Analyzing the Business Situation

- Business Profit and Loss Dynamics
- Financial, Marketing and Behavioral Goals
- Strengths, Problems, Opportunities and Threats (SPOT)

BOX IV

Designing Action Programs and Monitoring Systems

- Communications Mix
- Product Programs
- Monitoring and Research Systems

BOX III

Examining Alternative Strategies

- Competitive Advantage
- Target Markets and Positioning
- Product, Price, Place and Promotion

"Where is the venture now?", "Where do I want it to go?" and "How am I going to get it there from here?" These are the questions you want answered if this book is to be worth reading. An analytic business planning tool, called the *4-Box Model,* is used throughout this book as a way of understanding where your venture is now. (See Figure I.2.) It is developed in Part 1, "A New Beginning," as a way to reanalyze your business as you begin to plan your journey of rapid growth.

Chapters 1 and 2 provide the foundation for the ongoing analysis of your venture's environment, its current business situation and your role within it. These chapters outline a framework and questions to be answered for you to understand where your venture is now and where you want it to go.

Chapters 3 and 4 take the analysis of the environment and business situation several steps further—to how you get there from here. You need to apply the analyses conducted in these chapters to the growth aspects of the business. As you master the thought processes that go into the frameworks suggested in these first four chapters, you will integrate them into your style of learning-by-doing.

WHAT'S AHEAD?

As rapid growth continues, the need for operating mechanisms and controls increases. New venture managers often have difficulty delegating and letting go of critical decisions. More importantly, they may not be able to determine when to draw on their entrepreneurial skills versus when to develop their leadership skills. New ventures need strategic thinking and leadership; more entrepreneurship without these new skills being added will not lead to accelerated growth and profitability.

David, an owner of a coffee roaster and chain of retail coffee stores, reflects on his rapid growth situation: "I knew that I had something special; people would comment on the quality and taste of our coffees all the time. I decided to start a mail-order business to supplement the coffee store activity—this would allow for greater volume roasting and sales to support the increasing costs of capital.

"While the idea was a good one, and has turned out to be extremely successful, the process of entering into this additional business and expanding it rapidly nearly crippled the retail coffee house business. We did not have the ordering systems, warehousing or managers to run a second business. Fortunately, we changed fast enough to survive this expansion and prosper.

"I looked for a comanager, a partner really, to work the direct mail side of the business. I concentrated on what I knew best—coffee selection, blending and roasting. Our success four years later is obvious. But we learned most of what we now do well along the way."

The increase in the volume of business or the types of businesses conducted often alter the physical and mental activities needed to sustain rapid growth. Working longer days is rarely the solution. Hiring people, developing a sense of shared vision among employees and building operating systems to replace personal control are some of the changes that need to take place. Sound difficult? It is, but it is also exciting—just as starting and sustaining your venture has been up until now.

Every new venture manager's path to rapid growth is clouded by obstacles and opportunities. There are many ways to go and different things that one can accomplish; denial and focus are key. By learning to leverage what has been accomplished, the challenges of obtaining rapid growth and profit become manageable. For example, additional capital can often be obtained for a business because the venture's initial success has been demonstrated and survival is real. Past accomplishments can be leveraged to attract new financial resources. This often involves sharing equity and control of the venture with others.

As the activity levels within a venture increase to meet increased demand for the products and services offered, the information and control procedures in place will need to be updated, revised or entirely redone to reflect the increased volume and variety of activities. Accounts receivable collections may become a major issue as some buyers are delinquent in their payments and capital is needed for more inventory or staff.

As decisions will continue to be made quickly due to market and customer pressures, analysis will lag behind action. The number of surprises experienced by your venture's staff will increase dramatically as the number of contacts, relationships and transactions increases. Sound exciting? It is. Now let's turn that excitement toward your leadership of the process.

1

————————

Focusing on the Right Stuff

Much like the basic advice to stock investors (buy low, sell high), the advice to leaders of new ventures is equally simple and powerful: Know where you are now, know where you want to go and continually check to see if you are making progress towards getting there. Knowing this and doing this are not the same.

A few moments of reflection will help frame initial answers to some diagnostic questions.

————————

1. What are the distinctive competencies of your venture? What does your business do well now?

2. What critical things has it done to survive? List each one separately.

3. What were the key actions or events that created the foundation of your business?

4. What does your venture offer customers that is clearly distinct from what other businesses offer? What is its competitive advantage?

5. Which of your venture's distinctive competencies will persist as such for the next several years? Which will not?

6. Is the existing foundation (e.g., systems, infrastructure, equipment, people) capable of supporting rapid growth?

7. Is their capacity available for increased production, inventory, cash flow, leadership and people skills?

8. What needs to be done to create this capacity?

■──■

The answers to these questions are a point of departure. Yet, your initial answers are less important than the questions. *Learning to ask these questions* of yourself, your associates and your employees is critical to your venture's continued survival and will become critical to achieving rapid growth.

You may be thinking, Why are the questions more important than the answers? Edgar, the owner of a bicycle sales and service store, grappled with this idea as he watched his business dwindle in the midst of a consumer boom in bicycling. Edgar's answers to the previous questions six months earlier had led the business to its most profitable quarter. What had changed so fast that yesterday's success formula was today's ticket to nowhere?

I met Edgar on a chair lift while skiing. It was when we started talking about our professions that Edgar shared his new venture woes. He described his business situation and went on to say, "Two fashionable sporting goods stores opened within a mile radius of my shop. My walk-in business has all but stopped."

Edgar's business had lost its competitive advantage. He could not compete as a fashionable bike shop located on a side street off of a main roadway. When I asked Edgar what his business did well, he rattled off three or four things he did that the new competition was not likely to provide as a service to their customers.

By the time we reached the top of the mountain, Edgar had several ideas on how to proceed—each of which had promise for attracting the kind of customer that Edgar saw as his prime target. I recently learned that Edgar has opened up two additional bike shops, both on side streets, near schools that have a lot of bike traffic. Edgar is now in the bicycle accessories and maintenance business; sales of new bikes contribute less than 30 percent of the business revenues.

The eight questions suggested earlier are intended to guide your thinking. Your answers reflect what you think now. During periods of rapid growth, the answers may change in response to competitor activities, consumer behaviors and other environmental factors. The business situation changes sufficiently fast that answers to such questions during one quarter (which served to guide decisions and actions during that quarter) are imprecise or inappropriate the next quarter. New venture managers must overcome a natural tendency to hold on to an answer as if it were the solution to a math problem. There is little that is routine when growing a new venture rapidly.

A new venture's success indicates that its managers can and do learn by doing; they are astute and intuitive. They have found solutions to problems associated with start-up and survival. This is a strength of an entrepreneurial person that is less common in traditional managers who have come up through the ranks of large organizations. It is a strength that needs to be refined and leveraged as one seeks rapid growth. It is also a strength that many people do not have—and one that is particularly difficult to teach. Having this strength and applying it in new situations will require ongoing experimentation and learning from your actions.

This book will not teach you the ten steps to follow to obtain rapid growth and profits. Such steps do not exist. It can assist you in learning from your actions and inactions so that you can teach yourself how to achieve the growth in sales and profits you envision. To start the process, a framework is needed to organize the mountains of information and streams of ideas you have in your mind. No computer is needed here—just the brainpower you have been using each day applied within a framework that you can incorporate into your business life. The framework is called the 4-Box Model.*

THE 4-BOX MODEL—AN ANALYTIC FRAMEWORK FOR STRATEGIC THINKING

The model shown in Figure 1.1 has been used by thousands of people involved in new ventures to stimulate and guide their thinking. It provides a way to organize information and ideas so as to make them easier to access, understand and communicate. The model gets its name from the four primary tasks needed for effective strategic thinking: (1) assessing the

---

* An earlier version of the 4-Box Model was introduced to me by Dr. Dale Zand in 1977. Mr. Robert Longman and I revised the model in 1984. The research undertaken for *The Growth Challenge* has led to a number of subsequent changes.

Figure 1.1 The 4-Box Model—An Analytic Framework for Strategic Thinking

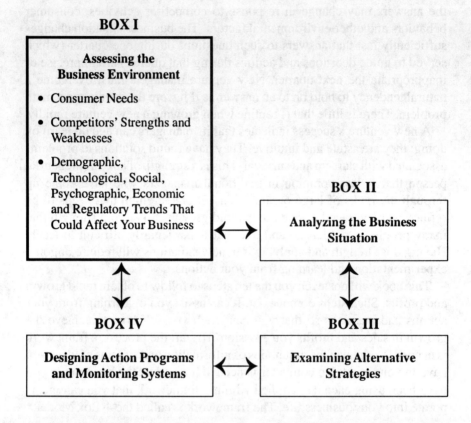

BOX I

Assessing the Business Environment

- Consumer Needs
- Competitors' Strengths and Weaknesses
- Demographic, Technological, Social, Psychographic, Economic and Regulatory Trends That Could Affect Your Business

BOX II

Analyzing the Business Situation

BOX IV

Designing Action Programs and Monitoring Systems

BOX III

Examining Alternative Strategies

business environment, (2) analyzing the business situation, (3) examining alternative strategies and (4) designing action programs and monitoring systems.

The analyses suggested by the four boxes and the bullet points therein are interdependent. The collection of information and your analysis of that information for the elements in Box I will affect your thinking as it relates to the other three boxes. Later, when you are deep in analysis of information in another area, your ideas will link and often force you to reevaluate the utility and results of your earlier analyses.

The ideas and analyses of the four boxes are dependent on each other. Expect to think one thing on one day based on your analysis of some aspects of your situation and to change your mind later on after considering other elements in your analysis. Both analyses may be useful and appropriate at the time. Neither will provide the single right answer to guide your actions for long during periods of rapid growth.

The process of using the 4-Box Model is intentionally *iterative,* as is the process of completing a crossword puzzle. With a crossword puzzle, you start where it is easiest for you, move to other answers that you think you know and sometimes return to an earlier part of the puzzle to make a change that at this later point in time seems a better answer than you provided earlier. While not a puzzle, the 4-Box Model is best viewed as a set of clues that you use iteratively to guide your thinking about your business. We discuss Box I here. Boxes II, III and IV are covered in chapters 2, 3 and 4, respectively. The interrelationships among the four boxes are discussed throughout subsequent chapters.

BOX I: ASSESSING THE BUSINESS ENVIRONMENT

For convenience, we start with the box in the upper left-hand corner—assessing the business environment. Each bullet in Box I signifies a critical area for issue diagnosis, analysis and understanding.

A new venture, like any fish in the ocean, has many different environments. The fish may see its environment as water, or water and photoplankton (food for many fish), or water, photoplankton, other fish, predators, sunken ships, algae, etc.

The "right" definition of the venture's environment, much like the fish's environment, depends on what external factors affect the venture over time as it tries to accomplish its goals. The environment will change for many reasons, most of which are outside of the venture's control. Some of the changes will adversely affect the business, other changes may have no effect on it and still other changes may benefit it.

Three areas of the business environment need particular attention: (1) consumer needs, (2) competitors' strengths and weaknesses and (3) trends that can affect the new venture. Failure to continually assess and reassess these aspects of the environment will hamper your business analysis and lower the quality of decisions based on such analyses.

CONSUMER NEEDS

What is the consumer need that the venture's product or service satisfies? Do customers really need this product or service? What would happen to the customers if it were not available? Is the product satisfying consumers' needs or customers' wants? Why are people buying the product? The answer to these questions is neither simple nor similar for all customers. Let's explore why.

Needs are the outcomes of basic drives common to all, or at least most, people. We all need food. You may want a pizza while I may want a hot fudge sundae. Both of these products may satisfy our need for food. Most people purchase what they want if it relates to some general need—one that could be satisfied by many different products or services. Most of us want to offer a product that satisfies a previously unmet need—for example, the cure for AIDS. But more than likely, our products satisfy some specific wants of a portion of the population that are or could be satisfied by other products.

This distinction between needs and wants may seem unnecessary. It is true that most people discuss their wants as needs. "We need a new television." "He needs new clothes." At this general level, a television or clothes may be a need that is being satisfied. But people do not buy just any television or purchase clothes from just any store or maker. They buy specific products based on a host of wants, some of which they do articulate. Many of the reasons for a particular purchase are based on wants of which the consumer is unaware; these wants are part of the consumer's subconscious. Yet both the conscious and subconscious wants drive purchase behavior. This is why some purchase decisions people make seem irrational, particularly when consumers purchase a competitor's product that we believe is clearly inferior to ours.

Martha expressed such a concern with respect to her garden shop. "Why do so many people buy their cut flowers and plants from Ghrishams? Our cut flowers last longer, look better and are priced just about the same. Our plants hold up much better than Ghrishams."

Martha found out later that the answer to her question was that Ghrishams provided a plant care instruction card and 800 phone number as part of their postpurchase service. The plant care instructions, which Martha often gave orally, were not always remembered. Access to an 800 number eased customers' concerns about how to keep their plants alive and healthy—even if they did not call the number.

Satisfy Customer Wants

Consumer indulgence in their wants suggests a different question than what consumers need. It suggests, *What do your customers want from you?* To grow a business, you will have to satisfy many more consumers than before (or the same customers more often)—either directly if you sell to the public or indirectly through middlemen, distributors, finished goods manufacturers and retailers.

Are you clear on the specific wants your product or service is satisfying for your customers? Have you asked the customers lately to verify your beliefs? Have you explored with your customers other possible wants they may have? A ten-minute conversation with 20 cooperative customers can identify important wants of which you may be unaware. Perhaps these less obvious wants will be the primary point of distinction between your products and the products of competitors six months from now.

Jason, the owner of a new copy shop thought he was satisfying his customers' needs for photocopies—and he was. When he asked his customers what else they wanted, he found out that quality binding of reports was important to them. With a $4,200 investment in high-quality binding equipment, Jason nearly doubled his sales and profits in three months.

If you want a continuous increase in sales, your venture has to be satisfying the wants of customers before its competitors do. The more subtle the want being satisfied, the more transparent that want will be to your competitors until they get as smart as you are.

A subtle want does not necessarily mean a weak preference. Many people prefer Coca-Cola over Pepsi or Miller Lite over Bud Light with passion, but their preference is based on subtle factors. These factors are often unrelated to consumers' stated taste preferences. (Witness the results of most blind taste tests: the majority of people cannot distinguish a difference in taste between their preferred product and a leading competitor's product.) For consumer products like soda and beer, the subtle factors most likely relate to how people feel about themselves when they consume the beverage. The consumption of branded products, particularly in public, carries with it a sense of self that may be difficult to articulate but easy to experience.

A second question to consider with respect to consumer wants is, *Why do they want it from you?* While a product or service offered by a new venture may be unique, it generally is not the only product that can satisfy customers' needs. There are many substitutes for nearly every product or service available today. If a product is unique and in demand, it will not remain unique for long. New product and service ideas get copied quickly due to the existence of a global economy and the difficulty of proving and litigating against those believed to be infringing on the product owner's rights.

Why do customers satisfy their wants through purchase of your venture's product? Is it price, product quality or service quality? Is it a prestigious retail location or the convenience of a location? Is it the product's technical specifications, versatility, payment terms, ease of ordering or what?

Many a lemonade stand has gone out of business by assuming that people were buying lemonade because they wanted lemonade. When iced tea became available half a block away, some lemonade businesses learned that their consumers were satisfying their want for a refreshment. Others learned that their customers primarily wanted a convenient location, taste or another factor that competitors were now providing to draw their customers away. Had the lemonade stand owner known that customers were buying convenience and refreshment, they might have relocated and offered iced tea as well. Why do your customers buy the products offered? Keep asking this question to identify and refine your understanding of each sale.

Avoid What Consumers Don't Want

Now that you are exploring why consumers want your product, *what is it about your product that they don't want?* Consumers sometimes have difficulty explaining why they want what they want. They provide an answer to the questions asked, but the answer may be a fleeting thought or a socially appropriate one, not a belief that is acted upon. Try asking what it is that they don't want. What don't they like about your product, service, location, size, shape, etc.? People are eager to share their criticism if they know there is no personal risk involved. Give them the opportunity and listen carefully to their responses.

Once you know their concerns, you may be able to do something about those concerns. Once you know what consumers don't want, you can choose whether or not to give it to them. Many product and service innovations in the 1970s and 1980s focused on what consumers did not want, with the success of the product being that it did not give it to them. Consider products such as diet colas and other diet beverages and foods, light and low-alcohol products and all those "low and no" products—low or no cholesterol, low or no fat, low or no sodium, low or no nicotine, no preservatives, no artificial flavors or colors and so forth.

The don't-give-it-to-them-because-they-don't-want-it idea has also affected many service industries. There have been efforts to reduce the line-wait time (consumer banking, grocery stores) and to provide more low-service or self-service lines as an alternative to the higher cost and greater time required to receive personalized service (e.g., the self-serve lines at gas stations and shuttle air service between New York and Boston or Washington, D.C.). Fast-food restaurants have taken some of the wait out of dining out. From a consumer wants point of view, find out what it is in your product and its delivery that consumers don't want and try not to give it to them.

Estimate Market Size

With a growing knowledge of what consumers and buyers want and do not want in the product and service offering, new venture managers need to determine how many customers are out there. Just how big is the market the venture is serving or intends to serve? It may be that the wants the venture's products satisfy well are not wanted by enough people to sustain rapid growth. Sure, many people could use the product, and it would benefit them. But that does not mean that they want it, that they want to buy it from you or that they have the energy and other resources to do so. Rapid growth is unlikely if the venture can not identify and reach a market 100 times the size of the market it is now serving.

Research suggests that for most new ventures that have survived the start-up stage, there are still many reachable consumers. In interviews with dozens of new venture managers, only a few felt that they had penetrated more than 2 percent of their reachable market after three years of sales. Most believed that 99.5 percent of their reachable market still had not tried their product or service and that most of the consumers would not recall their name if asked. Consumer knowledge and recall of your product is likely to be low. This must change.

Thinking about Your Consumers' Needs

To better understand the consumer needs that your venture's products satisfy, note some responses to the following questions:

- What are the key consumer or client wants being satisfied by our products? List each product separately.

- What substitute products seem to satisfy the same consumer wants?

- How is our product different?

- How can we link this difference to what the consumers want?

- What *don't* our customers or clients want?

- What can we do to not give it to them?

- How large is the market for our products? Realistically, how many potential customers or clients exist?

- What would be their likely usage or consumption pattern?

- Is demand for the products growing, stable or declining? At what annual rate of change?

- How many people are currently buying our products?

- How many people are in the market for our product or substitute products each week?

■──■

Edgar's Bike Shop

These questions are not easy to answer, nor do the answers necessarily remain the same for many years. Edgar, the bicycle shop owner mentioned earlier, answered the questions this way after he had opened his second shop.

- What are the key consumer or client wants being satisfied by our products?

   My customers are predominantly young people who use bikes for transportation or entertainment. When they come to the shop, they want replacement parts or accessories. If they want replacement parts, they may also want to borrow tools and equipment, or they may want one of the staff to repair a bike for them. The other thing that they want is to be able to leave their bikes at the shop before school, or early in the day, and to pick them up later that day.

- What substitute products seem to satisfy the same consumer wants?

   People can buy many of the same parts as I sell at other shops, but no service comes with the parts. I do have a few special accessories that sell well because others do not carry them; but for the most part, my largest selling items are available at stores like Western Auto, Sears and Herman's.

- How is our product different?

  The main differences are in the assistance we provide in assembly. We have tools available that can be signed out at no cost with a $10.00 deposit. We store bikes on our premises at no charge. And, we meet our completion times. If we commit to a 3:00 P.M. completion time, we meet it. We have even delivered bikes back to their owners at no charge if it is within ten blocks.

- How can we link this difference to what the consumers want?

  Our business started to boom when we started advertising the nature of our service. When our message was "get your new bike here," business was slow. As we began to position ourselves as the local service and repair shop, bikes came out of the woodwork to be repaired and accessorized.

- What *don't* our customers or clients want?

  People do not want a hassle—which is what they say they get at the larger stores that sell bikes. They also do not want to be inconvenienced. A bike is not their only means of transportation or entertainment. If it becomes too much of a hassle, they simply stop using it.

- What can we do to not give it to them?

  I have had to add staff and train people on bicycle repair and service quality. At first it was difficult to find qualified workers. My head was into looking for younger people—say, 14 to 18 years old—who could not get other employment easily. But this group couldn't work the hours I needed most—which were 7:00 A.M. to 2:00 P.M.

  A friend suggested that I consider hiring retired people, particularly the early retirees that seemed to have too much time and energy on their hands. I recruited people through my sister-in-law, who works at a beauty salon. She passed the word on to several of her customers, and they sent their husbands in for the job. Without this source of interested and competent labor, I could not have expanded.

- How large is the market for our products? Realistically, how many potential customers or clients exist?

  This is never going to be big business, but the local market is good. Most families have at least one bike; many have two or three. Each bike shop draws from approximately a one-mile radius, or about 5,000 families. This yields about 7,000 to 9,000 bikes to service. Once we have a customer, we see them about once a month. There is still plenty of potential out there, as our shops handle about 50 customers on weekdays and double that on weekends.

- What would be their likely usage or consumption pattern?

  As I mentioned, the younger customers come in early in the day and about once a month. Housewives, mothers and small children typically come in the mornings between 9:30 and 11:30. The serious cyclists come in after their workday or on weekends.

- Is demand for the products growing, stable or declining? At what annual rate of change?

  Demand for our service is growing due to the increasing number of people using bikes. From last year to this year we have more than doubled our business. Cycling is good exercise and cheap transportation. Lots of our customers are middle-class folk who go cycling rather than boating or swimming—it is so much more convenient.

- How many people are currently buying our products?

  We have about 1,000 customer names on file at each bike shop.

- How many people are in the market for our product or substitute products each week?

  That is a good question. As I mentioned, we estimate that there are up to 9,000 bikes in the neighborhood. But there could be many more. I'm going to look into this further.

Edgar's answers to these questions were provided during an hour-long conversation over coffee. He had not spent a lot of time preparing his answers, although he had thought about each question prior to our meeting. His answers are not meant to suggest or imply that there are right answers to these questions, as each venture will have unique answers. Edgar's answers are representative of the answers given by others as they begin to diagnose their customers' wants. With more complex products or new venture situations, the answers are often longer and themselves more complicated.

If such diagnostic questions are frequently answered, a venture can take actions that contribute to rapid growth. New venture managers look for problems to solve because it is exciting and satisfying to do so. Developing and updating one's understanding of consumer wants is an important aspect of finding new problems to solve.

COMPETITORS' STRENGTHS AND WEAKNESSES

A second area for assessment is the competition. Who are the venture's competitors? What other businesses are satisfying the same or similar wants? Such competitors are satisfying the wants of consumers who could, if provided a reason, use your product or service rather than theirs.

Only a small number of competitors will offer the same product or service to the same consumers that a successful new venture offers. If a market is already crowded, a new venture rarely survives start-up. Yet, having only a few direct competitors does not ensure rapid growth. Many potential customers will be having their wants satisfied by someone else when the new venture could be satisfying their wants instead. For example, movie theaters not only compete with other movie theaters offering the same or a different movie on a given day, but they compete with other forms of entertainment such as television, videos, books, plays, dance, eating at restaurants and even visiting friends. If theater owners are only seeking growth by attracting people who want to see the movie they are running on a given day, they'll never reach the sweet spot.

Marlboro Medium

The Philip Morris USA group within the Philip Morris organization recently introduced Marlboro Medium, a new cigarette designed to have more flavor than Marlboro Lights and less tar and nicotine than Marlboro. One could argue that they were the first to offer a "medium" cigarette. Alternatively, there are many cigarettes available that have more flavor than Marlboro Lights and less tar and nicotine than Marlboro. Has Philip Morris USA created a new product category without any competition (yet)? If there are competitors, who are they? Are they other Philip Morris brands or competitor brands such as Camel? How much market share is Marlboro Medium going to steal from Marlboro and Marlboro Lights?

To minimize the amount of cannibalizing its own brands, Philip Morris conducted extensive research on its competitors' products in the midrange of flavor and reduced levels of tar and nicotine. Their analysis suggested that while some cannibalization would occur, the bulk of the buyers of Marlboro Mediums would not be current Philip Morris brand smokers. Initial results suggest that their analysis and decision to offer Marlboro Medium was successful in increasing their cigarette sales.

Where does one draw the line when identifying the activities and products that comprise a new venture's competition? Should Philip Morris have considered the chewing tobacco competitors and even the chewing gum competitors in its analysis? Both of these products are alternative oral gratifiers.

The answer depends on how the venture plans to compete and the nature of the substitution of one product for another in the minds of the targeted consumers. Many new venture managers define their product too broadly (e.g., cigarettes as oral gratifiers) and the competition too narrowly (other cigarettes labeled "medium"). Their start-up experiences lead them to define the wants their products are satisfying in vague and general terms (people who want more flavor and less tar and nicotine). The feeling that "my product satisfies many wants" is often part of an entrepreneur's spirit. People should want it because it is new, improved and different.

In contrast to the broad definition of the consumer wants being satisfied, competition during the start-up stage is often defined by the new venture manager quite narrowly and precisely. Anyone who does not offer a product that has all of the features of the new product is not viewed as a real competitor. This narrow definition is myopic; it ignores those competitors that are providing substitute products.

A narrow definition of the competition may identify the most threatening competitors at the time a product is launched. As consumers and competitors become aware of the new product, the competitive field expands. One must return to this question: What wants are being satisfied by the new product, and when, where and how are consumers getting these wants satisfied? By answering questions that link the wants being satisfied to the product and competitor satisfying these wants, a more complete competitive environment can be identified. This broadened range of competitors needs to be examined with respect to the venture's growth goals, not its initial survival goals.

Thinking about Your Competitors' Strengths and Weaknesses

The objective of identifying competitors is to understand their strengths and weaknesses so as to be more effective in competing against them. While you may not be able to assess all of the strengths and weaknesses of each competitor, you can determine how the wants that you can satisfy for those consumers that you target are being satisfied by the competition. What is it about the video store down the street that attracts more people than Joe's theater on Tuesday nights? Why doesn't Joe go out and ask his target customers next Tuesday night? If Joe can understand how the same want is being satisfied by different competitors, he will be better able to take actions to attract some of the consumers to his business rather than watch them patronize a competitor.

Margaret did just this with her residential real estate business. She interviewed people she knew were using alternative agencies to find out what wants they were having fulfilled by others. To her pleasure, she determined that most competitors were not doing anything more than she was; consumers often found their realtors by chance within the general neighborhood in which they were interested in locating (or leaving). This suggested to Margaret the importance of an informal network within the community and of sharing information with others about her business activity.

Margaret set about getting her name and role as a real estate agent in front of more people. She attended many local functions, meetings, interest group activities and the like that she could identify. She enjoyed listening to people talk about their issues and concerns. When it was time to leave, she gave those she was with her business card and encouraged them to stop buy her office when they had time. In less than six months, Margaret's business was booming. She hired three new agents and has trained each of them to make the rounds in the community at least once each month. Visibility is key. Competitors that have visibility in Margaret's community seem to outperform those who may have more competency but little visibility.

Read the following questions and take a few minutes to list your venture's key competitors and some of their attributes.

- Who are the venture's competitors?

- Which competitors attract the bulk of our targeted customers?

- Where are they located?

- Who do they target with their products or services?

- What amount of sales do we lose to them each week? Why?

- What consumer wants are being satisfied?

- What are our competitors' strengths?

- What are they doing sufficiently well to attract consumers that could be our customers if they did not have their wants satisfied by competitors first?

Now look at the competition in a different way. A new venture has some reliable and satisfied customers. Why?

- What amount of sales does each competitor lose to us each week due to our ability to satisfy customers' wants better than they do?

- Which competitor weaknesses can we exploit without creating undo rivalry?

- How might competitors respond to our efforts to exploit these weaknesses?

- How can we protect the venture from retaliation by each competitor?

- How might we attract our competitors' best customers?

- Where do we need to expand our activities to satisfy more of the wants of our competitors' customers?

Much like the assessment of consumer wants, the assessment of competitors' strengths and weaknesses provides a foundation from which to grow a new venture. But what if you do not have the information necessary to answer all of these questions? Will the lack of such information prevent rapid growth?

This is the wrong question to be pondering. Achieving rapid growth requires a substantial increase in demand for the venture's products as well as the ability to satisfy that demand. New venture managers can attempt to stimulate *primary demand,* that is, create more demand for their product by encouraging more consumers to want more of what they have to offer. *Or, they can assess what consumers are getting from competitors, with the goal of providing enough distinctiveness in their product (including its service, location, etc.) to have consumers satisfy their wants through them rather than the competition, including businesses that offer substitute products.*

More new businesses that succeed focus on attracting people who want what they have to offer than do new businesses that try to change the wants of the consumer into what they offer. It is easier to get people to move their feet (or finger) to contact or respond to you when they already want what you offer than it is to influence their wants first and then get them to act. Knowing which competitors attract the bulk of your new venture's target consumers provides direction for your business efforts. It can assist you in determining the strength of the venture's competitive advantage and where more effort is needed to build and sustain that advantage.

TRENDS THAT COULD AFFECT THE BUSINESS

The third component of assessing the business environment is to identify trends that could affect the new venture. Trends, if identified and sustained over the forecast period, can provide insight into the future. Most new ventures that are successful are riding one or more trends. The growth in consumer banking followed economic trends (increasing disposable income) and demographic trends (an aging population that has greater discretionary income) as well as social trends (dual-career families). The growth in health-oriented products followed the trends of greater health and fitness consciousness and an aging society. The packaging of itineraries for vacations followed the trend of the affluent to buy these services rather than commit their time to planning a vacation. It is much easier to ride a trend—that is, provide a product or service that is already part of the wants of the consumer—than it is to buck a trend or to create a trend.

What trends are likely to affect your business? Think broadly. Are the changes in the economy, regulation or technology that are discussed in magazines, newspapers and on television going to affect your business? In what ways and how soon? The health and fitness trend has certainly affected the success of many new products. Are there more subtle changes in demography (i.e., age, gender, family patterns, living arrangements), society or personal beliefs and attitudes (psychographics) that might affect the demand for your venture's products?

Consider the trend toward "ecologically correct" behavior. How might this trend affect your business? There is an interest group that researches and reports on the ecological correctness of different products. When this self-created group obtained media attention, they commented on the ecological correctness of several consumer products. Kraft products were given a lower ecological rating than some of its competitors. And why did their products get a lower rating? Because Kraft is owned by Philip Morris, and Philip Morris is not considered to be sufficiently ecologically correct. While there may not be many consumers who change their purchase behaviors as a function of these ratings today, this could change over the next decade. It was less than ten years ago that only a few food manufacturers were concerned about the amount of cholesterol in their products. Today most are.

Extrapolating Current Trends

One way to expand your contemplation of trends and how the behaviors suggested by a trend may affect a business is to explore the effects of some current trends on your business. While you might hire someone who is an expert on trends to assist you in analysis, there are books and magazines that regularly try to identify trends affecting business and society. For example, Faith Popcorn's *The Popcorn Report* (Doubleday, 1991) identifies social and psychographic trends that her firm's research suggests will affect various products by the year 2010.

A second way to explore trends is to look at what exists today and ask, *What if this continues and becomes popular?* Charles Handy did just this in his book *The Age of Unreason* (The Harvard Business School Press, 1989). The value of trend prediction is in predicting the future. If new venture managers can identify a trend before competitors do, they may be able to satisfy the wants of a larger share of the consumers following that trend. Nike beat Converse in identifying the trend of consumers' wants for sports shoes that were technologically superior. Miller effectively marketed a Lite® beer before Anheuser-Busch for the weight-conscious beer drinker. Bic captured much of the disposable pen and mechanical pencil markets before Scripto or Parker responded to the consumers' desire for low-cost, moderate-quality writing instruments.

Thinking about Trends That Could Affect the Business

What trends is your business trying to leverage? Consider the following questions:

- How is technology affecting our business? Is it in production? Delivery? Payment systems? Operating systems? Inventory control? Quality control? Personnel management? Marketing methods?

- What social and demographic trends are affecting consumer wants for our products? How?

- What economic trends are affecting the marketplace for the type of product we offer?

- Will the trend affect all competitors equally?

- How can we stand out from the masses?

- Are there legal or regulatory trends or events that could affect our business? State actions? Local government actions? Federal actions? Agencies such as OSHA or EPA?

- Are there groups of people that have declared interests that could affect our business (e.g., Mothers Against Drunk Drivers, Right to Life, The Ecologically Correct, etc.)?

- Are there psychographic trends that could affect the business?

- Are consumers changing the way they think or what they value in predictable ways?

Having reflected on the business environment, let's take a closer look at one new venture's business environment—the residential mortgage business for a commercial bank.

THE RESIDENTIAL MORTGAGE NEW VENTURE ENVIRONMENT

The massive failures of savings and loan institutions in the 1980s created opportunities for commercial banks and insurance companies to enter the residential mortgage market (mortgages on single-family homes, cooperatives and condominiums). Up until this time, the majority of home mortgages were booked (and often held) by savings and loan institutions, credit unions, mortgage companies and community banks. As some of these institutions faltered, commercial banks and insurance companies entered the residential mortgage market with clear goals for rapid growth (e.g., Prudential Insurance, Travelers Insurance, Bank of America and Security Pacific).

One financial institution, fictitiously called Financorp, established the following mission for its residential mortgage business about two years after entering the market:

> The mission of Residential Mortgage is to establish Financorp as the driving force and lender of choice in the California mortgage market by

- developing a highly professional, customer-driven organization;
- delivering an ongoing stream of superior products and services; and
- producing significant profits for the organization.

Financorp summarized its business environment in the following ways.

Mortgage Customer Needs and Dynamics

Looking forward, it is likely that the consumer will become an increasingly more important force in the mortgage market. Nearly 30 percent of all consumers investigate their main banks for mortgage rates before closing their mortgages. As we begin to explore direct-to-consumer distribution options, understanding consumers' needs is critical to the ultimate success of our efforts. Below we discuss several factors that seem to shape consumers' decisions and identify several consumer segments that offer opportunities for targeted products and/or marketing programs.

In selecting a mortgage supplier, consumers display a number of characteristics that differ significantly from the ways that mortgage intermediaries make their decisions. On the whole, consumers are

- heavily reliant upon others, such as REALTORS® or mortgage brokers, for advice on whom to approach for a mortgage and how to go about doing so;
- willing to shop around for the best rate;

- very concerned about being turned down, particularly first-time borrowers;
- committed to their choice once they have selected their mortgage supplier; and
- apparently beginning to reassess their reliance on mortgage brokers.

Competitive Analysis

One of Financorp's greatest strengths lies in its strong and widespread indirect distribution system—a system we must continue to leverage in the face of significant challenges from our competitors. For Financorp, the competitive environment is an increasingly difficult one. Our market share has decreased over the past year due to the following three factors:

1. Higher rates than competitors, particularly with adjustable rate mortgages

2. Aggressive activity by competitors

3. Less differentiation in distribution systems or service than in previous years

Compounding the issue, Financorp is now competing with a new, formidable set of competitors: other commercial banks and insurance companies. These entities have deep pockets, apparent long-term commitment to investing in the market and the ability to replicate our service advancements quickly. Finally, the coming year will bring additional challenges as competitors bring new technologies to market. These new technologies could threaten the distinctiveness of our offering.

Distribution System Strengths. As we look at our competitive situation, we conclude that our MortgageForce program is one of our greatest strengths, and one that we must leverage to the fullest. We are somewhat more dependent on the indirect channel than some of our competitors, reflecting our strategic focus on building our MortgageForce network. Here is how we stand vis-à-vis our competitors:

- Prudential Insurance—100 percent indirect sourced

- *Financorp*—94 percent indirect sourced

- Travelers Insurance—93 percent indirect sourced

- Bank of America (B of A)—90 percent indirect sourced

- Security Pacific—75 percent indirect sourced

Today our active membership consists of 1,043 intermediaries. The bulk of these are either real estate brokers or mortgage brokers. The numbers break down as follows: mortgage brokers, 40 percent; real estate brokers, 31 percent; attorneys and CPAs, 12 percent; private banking, 13 percent; and financial advisors, 4 percent. Although our business is somewhat concentrated, we are not dependent on a small number of brokers for the majority of our business—a situation that reduces our vulnerability.

Rate Disparity.   Several factors contributed to our slow growth last year. One cause lies in the distinctly higher rates that, until recently, we were charging for our products. In particular, our adjustable rate mortgage (ARM) product rates were significantly higher than the overall market. Our MortgageForce members report that this rate differential is the primary reason why they referred business elsewhere.

Most Important Problem Financorp Faces	Most Important Reasons Clients Chose Other Banks
High rates—68%	Lower rates—35%
Poor service/underwriting—32%	Better service/underwriting—30%
Poor products—16%	Better products—10%

Entry by Aggressive Competitors.   Another cause of slow growth lies in the entry and aggressive activity from a new, formidable set of competitors. The market has seen a proliferation in the number of formal lender-intermediary networks. This has reduced our differentiation in the marketplace. The market is beginning to be dominated by MortgageForce clones, who have registered the largest share gains.

An additional challenge to our position has come from aggressive competition from commercial banks, who have proven to be formidable competitors for the following reasons:

- Strong balance sheets and considerable financial clout
- Resources and know-how to replicate competitors' products and marketing/service tactics quickly
- Strong desire to be in the market; attractive balance-sheet implications due to changes in capital asset requirements; opportunity for significant profits
- Broad depositor base to target

- Broad consumer name recognition and strong reputations

Loss of Service Differentiation. Finally, a contributor to our slow growth is our loss of service superiority over our competition, particularly against MortgageForce "clones." According to industry surveys, Financorp is only at parity with key lenders when ranked on service delivery overall. In particular, there is only one service feature—expertise of sales force—in which Financorp leads the competition.

Trends That Could Affect the Residential Mortgage Business

In the past year Financorp has made significant improvements in the way they do business. This does not mean that they can allow themselves to become complacent. Indeed, the coming year promises to bring major challenges as market forces shift and competitors become even stronger. The increase in credit problems, particularly with broker-sourced mortgages, needs to be reflected in the way they do business. As they entered the new year, Financorp identified the following trends.

1. Mortgage demand will be off, dropping 4 percent below current-year levels. Demand will be adversely affected by a continuation of relatively high mortgage rates, a slower-growing local economy and, most profoundly, the inability of many families to afford homes.

2. Consumer needs will provide opportunity for new products and marketing programs aimed at specific segments (e.g., an effective jumbo/superjumbo mortgage offering aimed at the affluent market). Moreover, as we analyze changes in consumer behavior, we see that the possibility of direct-to-consumer sourcing is becoming an increasingly real possibility. We must prepare ourselves for what could amount to a revolution in the way we do business by beginning to develop products, programs and, most importantly, service delivery systems that will allow us to serve the direct market better than our competitors.

3. Regulatory issues will not claim the attention they demanded last year. The RESPA threat is currently quiet while Congress directs its attention to the FSLIC reform legislation. Two other proposals are of interest: (1) the possibility that Congress will allow retirement fund savings to be used as a down payment for a home and (2) the threat that limits may be set on the amount of deductible mortgage interest. We also hope that FHA loan limits will be increased.

4. Distribution channels will continue to be dominated by intermediaries in the near term, underscoring the need to strengthen and broaden our relationships with this channel via improved relationship management and other service capabilities. The need for superior service delivery is all the more urgent because our distribution channels have been gaining power at the expense of lenders. We trace this power shift to two factors: (1) consolidation of business in the hands of fewer intermediaries and (2) the growth in the number of formal lender-intermediary programs that allow the indirect channels to pick and choose among leaders.

5. The *competitive environment* will be increasingly challenging as we fight to take market share from sophisticated, tenacious competitors. Competition is strong because of rate/product disparity (rates and product benefits are not always easy to compare among competitors), aggressive activity by an emerging set of formidable competitors and less distinction in our service offering.

ASSESSING YOUR BUSINESS ENVIRONMENT

As the previous analysis of the residential mortgage business from Financorp's perspective suggests, assessing the environment is a critical part of determining how to grow a business rapidly and profitably. Financorp's environmental analysis laid the groundwork for their competitive strategy and marketing activities, which together led to both rapid growth and profits in the year that followed.

Having explored some of the questions suggested earlier as they relate to your business's environment, you have begun the process. You will need to return to these questions, and the answers you have considered, as you lead the venture. The more you can perform an ongoing diagnosis of your business environment, the greater the chance of leading the business toward that sweet spot. One cannot expect to develop a capacity to think strategically—to assess hundreds of issues, ideas and events, synthesizing them into meaningful actions—without practice. This may be the only practice opportunity that you permit yourself. The payoff is great, the cost modest.

2

Taking Inventory

When Hurricane Andrew swept through the Southeast, most people had been warned, did what preparation they could and battled the storm as was necessary. This is a bit of what it is like during the start-up of a new venture or when launching a new product. There is a lot of turbulence in the environment; powerful forces are present, but their effects are not entirely predictable; and the results of your efforts may, or may not, lead to survival. As the storm ends, the turbulence settles down, and the process of putting things in order begins. This is where you are now.

BOX II: ANALYZING THE BUSINESS SITUATION

Having survived the start-up stage, new venture managers need to assess their business to determine where it needs maintenance, rebuilding, restocking and management attention. As shown in Figure 2.1, this involves analyzing the business situation by (1) reviewing the venture's profit and loss dynamics; (2) re-establishing financial, marketing and behavioral goals in light of the venture's new potential; and (3) leveraging certain strengths to solve critical problems while seeking high-yield opportunities and minimizing the risk of threats that can lead to losses.

BUSINESS PROFIT AND LOSS DYNAMICS

You can never know too much about how your business generates revenues and expenses. Since it is a new business, some of the assumptions

Figure 2.1   Box II of the 4-Box Model—Analyzing the Business Situation

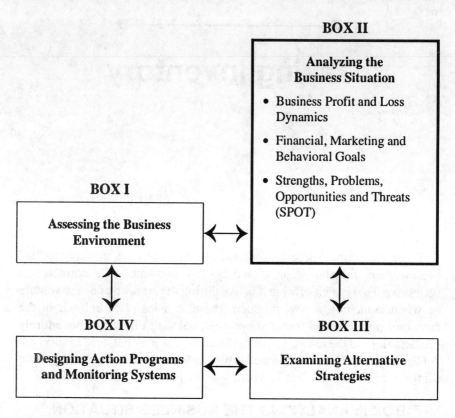

made in the initial business proposal have turned out to be accurate; others have proven to be inaccurate. Some of the revenue and expense relationships used to generate the pro forma profit and loss statement still make sense, others have not held up. But which ones are which? It is necessary to review the details of the business P&L to re-establish and revise your understanding of how the business *really* makes and spends money.

When I ask new venture managers about the profit and loss dynamics of their business, I am generally shown the business plan, an income statement and their accounting and sales records. As a newcomer to their business, this information provides me with a sense of what others view are the critical aspects of the business for planning and reporting purposes. With this information in hand, I have found a more useful set of questions to ask.

Thinking about Your Business Profit and Loss Dynamics

Consider the following questions for your business:

- How do we make money in our business? What are the three largest revenue streams?

- On what do we spend money in our business? What are the three largest expense categories?

- What financial ratios are key to this product and industry?

- What operating ratios are key?

- What is the industrywide average rate of return for this product and market?

- What does a customer have to do for the venture to make money?

- What must a customer *not* do in order for us to keep the money we thought we had made?

- What do our employees need to do for the venture to make money from customers?

- What must our employees *not* do for us to keep the money we thought we had made?

- How can these factors be managed? What changes are feasible?

These questions get at the *dynamics* of the business—that is, the aspects of the business that are variable and must be understood and continually managed for revenues to be generated and expenses controlled. Of course, there are revenue and expense sources beyond the largest three asked for in the previous questions. And there are expenses other than those associated with employees' contacts with customers, such as the interest on loans or rental fees for equipment, office space, production facilities and warehouses and the purchasing of raw materials, office supplies and so on. While new venture managers may hire accountants and bookkeepers to track these expenses, understanding them is still the venture manager's responsibility.

Ratio Analysis

In most businesses there are expected relationships between key financial and operating indicators, such as sales and expenses or inventory and demand for the product. These relationships tend to be rather constant over time as they reflect the underlying structure of the industry in which the venture competes. Years of experience by others in the same or similar businesses have left tons of information on annual profits, sales revenues, inventory sizes, head counts, administrative expenses, marketing expenses, advertising and the like. This information is analyzed by trade associations each year to identify key relationships, generally presented in the form of financial and operating ratios for businesses of a particular size in each industry segment covered by the industry association.

Financial and operating ratios suggest what has been achieved in terms of cost and revenue relationships and what might best be sought (or not sought) given the historic structure of the business. Most trade associations publish such reports on the historical financial and operating relationships of their respective industries. William Cohen presents a list of trade associations in his book, *The Entrepreneur & Small Business Problem Solver.*

A few examples of financial relationships will suggest their usefulness. For retail businesses dealing with foods and household goods, such as green grocers and corner stores, labor costs of the more successful businesses run no more than 10 percent of revenues. Grocery stores operate on a thin profit margin—often less than 10 percent of revenues. If labor costs are 15 percent or higher, the venture will not be adequately profitable to survive economic or market downturns.

The ratios of interest are quite different in the publishing industry. Labor (including royalties to authors) and marketing costs are a high percentage of the total costs; production costs for most books are less than 15 percent of the book's list price. For mass-market books written by established authors that are intended to yield volume sales, production costs may be as low as 8 to 10 percent. It is hard to believe that the last book you bought for $24.95 probably cost the publisher less than $3.00 per copy to typeset and print. The author probably received less than $2.00 for each copy sold.

The person who should *seriously* track profit and loss dynamics is the new venture manager. Do not rely on an accountant to do this. Accountants are trained to focus on information needed and used for reporting purposes. By the time an accountant identifies a problem, it is too late.

Are you familiar with the key ratios in your business? What are they? Why are they key? Might these ratios change as the venture expands and attains accelerated growth? Of course the venture will get the benefit of having its fixed costs spread over a larger sales base. That you know. It is what you have yet to find out about the changing profitability dynamics and financial ratios that is critical to your venture's future success. An example will highlight this point.

Maureen—A Training Materials Vendor

Maureen was running a training materials operation that provided a group of independent consultants with materials for management development programs. The consultants would have their clients pay a materials fee and royalty for the training materials that were needed for a program. As the operation grew, the "just-in-time" production process that was in place at start-up needed to be augmented with an inventory of supplies—raw materials as well as finished products. The cost of carrying the inventory, theft and damaged goods losses, and out-of-date materials in the inventory added to the costs of operations.

These were small problems relative to the decrease in flexibility in the packaging of materials that occurred. Inventories of finished goods were partially assembled. When a consultant wanted materials tailored to a client's needs, it often meant disassembly followed by reassembly. Of course this was not always done in a timely and error-free manner. Added to this problem was the challenge of a growing number of programs that required unique materials or special assembly.

The result was the loss of sales and a growing sense of dissatisfaction among the independent consultants regarding the products and services they were receiving. Some began to seek alternative suppliers. The cost of correcting the problem involved a stronger quality control effort, greater customer service and responsiveness after a sale and the training of new employees.

Had the materials and royalty fees been price-inelastic or under contractually bound prices, the operation would have begun to lose money just as its sales growth rate was increasing. Through analyzing the profitability dynamics of the business in light of the administrative and market changes taking place, Maureen decided to raise prices. The clients responded well to the increased service and lower error rates, and profits followed revenues.

Of course, for those who regularly examine and reexamine the profitability dynamics of their businesses, this sounds like Business 101. For those who wrote your business plan and have subsequently assumed it to be a valid representation of your business, it is time to examine the profitability dynamics again. In all likelihood the profitability dynamics have changed— at least that is the understanding of 75 percent of the new venture managers with whom I have worked.

FINANCIAL, MARKETING AND BEHAVIORAL GOALS

The importance of goals is a rarely contested concept in business and the behavioral sciences. When goals are specific, clear and accepted by those whose behavior the goals are intended to influence, more tends to be accomplished in the direction provided by the goal than if no goal existed. Goals are meant to direct and motivate people by identifying desired results and behaviors. Goals do not replace the skill, knowledge or training needed to perform effectively. Having a goal from the start is more likely to result in people doing something to accomplish that goal.

Goals become powerful motivators of behavior when measures are used that accurately reflect the extent of goal accomplishment and when people receive feedback on their performances that relate to the goals. If you can couple goal accomplishment with feedback, rewards and praise, you have a winning combination.

The remaining task is to ensure that you establish goals that are sufficiently difficult to be challenging. Very difficult goals tend to demoralize people to the point of not trying. Alternatively, people quickly lose interest in accomplishing easy goals—to the point of not bothering.

Some of the questions that relate to establishing goals asked by new venture managers include "How much direction is needed?" "How specific should the goals be?" "How many goals should be established?" "What are the best measures of goal accomplishment?" Such questions are best answered in light of the business profit and loss dynamics. By identifying the key areas of activity that generate revenues, you can establish meaningful goals that link directly to the behaviors desired and develop measures to assess goal accomplishment. A parallel set of goals can be established for behaviors you want to influence with respect to expenses.

Greg and Alice tackled the goals issue directly in their dry cleaning and laundry business. They had inherited the business with its $1,200,000 in revenue from their uncle. Unfortunately, they knew little about the business, and it was not earning much profit. Their initial thought was to sell it, but before doing so, they sought some expert advice.

After examining how the dry cleaning and laundry business makes money, they decided to run it for one year before selling. They worked closely with their late uncle's staff to understand what goals were possible as well as what goals were unrealistic. Within six months, they had established goals for 23 areas of activity. The goals were difficult but not unreasonable. The goals were understood and accepted by those responsible for their accomplishment. By the end of their first year as owner-managers, they had improved the profitability of the firm by 320 percent—to a healthy 21 percent of revenues (which had increased to $1.45 million). In the subsequent three years, Greg and Alice have led the business to over $5 million in revenues. Profits still hover around 20 percent.

Goals rarely control behavior, but they often influence it. When someone gets confused due to too many or conflicting goals, a business loses the influence it sought when it established those goals. New ventures need as many goals as there are discrete critical behaviors that must be influenced. Too many goals bind people and stifle their creative thinking and independent problem solving. Too few goals may permit undesired discretion in critical areas or allow people to flounder due to lack of direction.

Financial and Marketing Goals

Most successful new venture managers have found ways to establish useful financial and marketing goals (e.g., reach $2,000,000 in sales by the close of the second quarter, increase sales next quarter by 28 percent or attain 2 percent of the market share by year-end). These goals reflect bottom-line accomplishments. They link directly to the income and expense reporting systems used by their accountants. Financial and marketing goals that link to the reporting system are particularly valuable to the constituencies that use this information (e.g., bankers, securities analysts, venture capital firms, shareholders) to evaluate the ongoing performance and viability of a venture.

Other types of goals—behavioral goals—are as important as financial and marketing goals but are often not considered prior to embarking on rapid growth. Behavioral goals specify the kind and level of behaviors that must occur to generate revenues or the behaviors that, as they occur, generate expenses.

Behavioral Goals—Peter's Specialty Magazine

Behavioral goals link human behavior to the business profit and loss dynamics through a venture's marketing and financial goals. For example, consider the following marketing goal: increase sales of our new halogen office lamp by 33 percent over the next three months. Such a goal might also reflect a financial goal: increase total revenues by $590,000 next quarter, or to $2,360,000.

There are apt to be some very specific behavioral goals that need to be accomplished for the sales and revenues to increase. Sales personnel will have to make sales calls, or direct mail and telemarketing efforts will have to be made. People must to do some things differently than before, and those changes must be successful.

The importance of behavioral goals, in the shadow of a venture's financial and marketing goals, is highlighted by Peter's development of a new specialty magazine. Peter, previously the editor of a small newspaper, decided to start a new venture to sell a specialty magazine that he would edit and publish. He had good contacts on the production side of the business but was less familiar with advertising sales and circulation issues.

The magazine would be given away free to about 12,000 professionals in the field that the magazine covered; all revenues were to be derived from advertising sales. In planning his selling effort, he worked backwards from his business plan and financial goal of $2.2 million in advertising revenues annually. He needed to determine how many pages of advertisements at what per-page fee would generate that figure. Since there were many possible answers, he studied several comparable magazines targeted to other professional specialties. He concluded that $2,000 per full-page ad was the most he could charge the first year.

Peter was beginning to move toward behavioral goals. He needed to sell about 100 pages of ads for each of the 12 issues annually. How many different advertisers existed? How many sales people would be needed to call on these advertisers of products and services?

To make this decision, Peter needed to estimate how many sales calls could be made per salesperson per week. Of these sales calls, he needed to know how many would be successful. It was by knowing (and learning) these dynamics of his business that he was able to establish meaningful behavioral goals.

Peter hired three salespeople to call on about 70 percent of the 558 potential advertisers. Each salesperson was given 130 accounts. Forty of these 130 accounts per salesperson ended up generating about 75 percent of all of the ads that ran in the magazine. It was necessary to make frequent sales calls because the products advertised changed every few months and new advertisers were always needed to fill space left blank by those firms not faring as well.

Peter established goals for the number of cold calls per week, the number of follow-up sales calls per week and the amount of ad space sold per week. Since most of these advertisers were located in other cities, he worked with the salespeople to establish goals for in-office time versus time on the road. The salespeople began thinking about how to best service the advertisers in light of these goals and their physical and personal constraints.

As people gained experience, the goals were adjusted to reflect what could be learned from the successful sales calls. Within six months, Peter and his people were achieving most of their goals each week. A new venture had survived start-up. In Peter's words, "It was setting and achieving specific sales call and dollar sales goals that made the difference. The salespeople knew what they had to do. If a goal turned out to be unreasonable, we worked backwards to find out why. On a few occasions we had established goals that placed someone on the road for 80 percent of the day while conducting sales calls only 20 percent of the time. This didn't work. We found that our best sales involved face-to-face contact for nearly an hour, so we used this knowledge to organize ourselves. The revised goals and operating plans worked better. They have been revised a few times since then, but the basic structure is now stable."

Peter has since created a family of magazines that target different professional specialties. Sales across this family of magazines, all of which are circulated free to professionals, have topped $10,000,000 in annual sales in three years. He has separate editors for each magazine and a total sales force of eight people. His salary is now well into six figures. His best salespeople do well financially as they can sell ad space for up to three of the six magazines he publishes. He provides no office space for the sales-people, but they have all been provided with cellular phones and laptop personal computers. Sales meetings take place at the office conference room weekly, and salespeople stop by the office as needed for supplies, discussions with Peter and/or the editors and morning coffee and Danish pastry. And the coffee is good!

Thinking about Your Financial, Marketing and Behavioral Goals

Since goals are expressions of what a venture wants, they should be easy to specify. What does a particular venture want to accomplish? Consider the following questions as you explore the things that your new venture wants to accomplish.

	Within 6 Months	Within 12 Months	Within 18 Months

- What do we want with respect to profits and ROI?
  Volume and growth?
  Market share?
  Product line extension?
  Spreading costs over a larger business base?
  Stability?
  Riskiness of investments?

- What are the actions required, and by whom, to reach each of these goals?

- What are our staffing and training goals?
  How many people need to be hired, at what level, and with what backgrounds and subsequent training?

STRENGTHS, PROBLEMS, OPPORTUNITIES AND THREATS (SPOT)

Developing an understanding of a new venture's strengths and capabilities is the third business area to analyze. Organizations and individuals perform more effectively when they are predominantly using established capabilities. This does not imply that new strengths should not be developed; rather, the development of new capabilities should consume a relatively small amount of energy so as not to distract the venture from leveraging existing strengths. This is particularly critical in periods of rapid growth because the venture has already moved away from a focus on entrepreneurism to a focus on productivity. The costs of developing new strengths is high relative to the cost of using a developed strength to achieve growth and profitability objectives.

Zach married an entrepreneur's daughter. Almost instantly he was involved in running one of his father-in-law's businesses—a garbage pickup service. He had become a "sanitation engineer" after four years of college and two years of teaching special education in the local primary school. While the prospects of his new job looked good, the image that his job carried was far from what he was seeking (or ever considered).

Within six months, Zach was in charge of the entire business: five trucks, three routes, and 20 employees. It was a multi-million dollar business already; his challenge was to double it in two years. But how?

Zach began to look for what the business was doing well already. Could they do more of that? Routes were very competitive; it would be difficult to get more routes. Alternatively, to take over more business on a route was possible. If enough business could be obtained, the other service provider on the route might sell off its remaining business. It was generally not profitable for a firm to collect on a route with less than 30 percent of the residences. Travel time was an expense, both in gasoline and in truck idle time.

Zach hired two salespeople to assist him in a door-to-door selling effort for all the residences on the route that his firm was not servicing. As a sales promotion, a garbage container was given to anyone who signed a one-year contract. Within six months Zach had attracted enough new business on one of the routes to drive out a competitor. He even paid handsomely for a competitor's truck as part of the buyout. By the end of the year, Zach was well on the way to doubling his business. What Zach had done, intuitively, was to focus on the business's strengths in order to seek a particular opportunity.

A widely used tool for conducting a capabilities analysis is SPOT (or SWOT). SPOT involves examining a business's strengths (S), problems (P) or weaknesses (W), opportunities (O) and threats (T). The SPOT model shown in Figure 2.2 encourages new venture managers to assess the capabilities of their business as part of a detailed analysis of the business situation.

SPOT does not replace other assessment tools such as MIS reports, accounting information or market research. Rather, the insights gained through the use of such assessment tools can be recorded on a SPOT chart as a way to present the analyses visually. SPOT is a diagnostic and discovery model whose four elements can collectively provide meaningful insights into which business actions are likely to be more viable.

The word *strengths* in the SPOT model is a label for those capabilities a new venture presently has. Each strength listed on the SPOT chart needs to be linked to the context in which it is a strength. For example, Levi Strauss is one of the worlds largest sellers of blue jeans. This may be a strength for the company in terms of name awareness in the jeans market. It is probably *not* a strength for Levi in the market for designer dresses. For a manager to state that Levi name awareness is a strength is not sufficiently precise to be useful; it may even be misleading. The Levi name is a strength in the jeans business; the company's name awareness is likely to be a strength for product lines that attract the same customers and/or have a comparable image as jeans. Strengths need to be identified with respect to the specific growth situation being pursued.

The value of examining *problems* is to identify those aspects of a new venture in which there are known gaps between where the business is now and where it was forecasted to be by now. A problem is something that one can choose to deal with by expending time and energy to solve or overcome it, or it may be something that one can choose to ignore. Identifying problems can lead to a reexamination of the goals and strengths of a business. Confronting the things that are not working out as intended leads managers to rethink previous decisions and actions, make changes and implement their ideas again.

Solving problems can be fun, but it can be frustrating as well. Some managers like the iterative nature of resolving problems, refinding them in a slightly different form and then solving them again. Others do not. Fortunately, not all problems need to be solved today or this week. The ability to sidestep some problems is a skill that the more successful new venture managers learn.

Figure 2.2   SPOT Chart for Analyzing the Business Situation

Strengths What does the venture do well now?	**Problems** What gaps exist between where the venture is now and where it was expected to be?
Opportunities What possibilities exist?	**Threats** What can go wrong?

Opportunities are the possibilities that exist in the future. There may be opportunities for opening new distribution channels, running a special sales promotion or improving a product's quality through a new manufacturing process. Some opportunities can be created by new venture managers when they have a strong sense of what they want and then find ways to achieve that goal. Other opportunities may be identified by peers and mentors, or they are suggested by others such as customers or competitors. Opportunities may also present themselves to whomever is at the right place at the right time. As you identify opportunities, they must be sorted or prioritized. Your task is one of choosing among the opportunities those that draw on your venture's strengths and are more likely to help the business accomplish its goals.

Threats are the things that can go wrong in the future. If things have already gone wrong, they are best viewed as problems. The value of distinguishing threats from problems is that problems are current issues that seem to demand attention, while threats are risks that may or may not materialize.

Managers can protect against threats by developing contingency plans, taking preventive steps to reduce the risk associated with a threat or avoiding high-risk opportunities. However, the threat must first be identified. It is often possible to identify and assess the level of a threat encountered by a business by asking for more information about the opportunities being considered and then exploring what can go wrong.

Financorp's Residential Mortgage Business SPOT Analysis

In chapter 1 we discussed the environmental assessment conducted by the new venture manager of the residential mortgage business at Financorp. Her business analysis included the SPOT summary shown in Figure 2.3.

Using a SPOT Analysis To Take Actions: The Residential Mortgage Situation

Based on this SPOT analysis and its understanding of the business environment, Financorp developed several programs to expand its business over 50 percent within the next nine months. Here is what they decided to do.

In the words of Financorp's new venture manager:

In determining how we will focus our efforts and energies, we have selected those areas that will have the most impact on building our business next year and beyond. The following four strategic thrusts have emerged:

1. Differentiate our service to our MortgageForce members via a relationship management approach to our business and the full implementation of MortgageForce PLUS.
2. Create targeted products and marketing programs aimed at key consumer segments.
3. Lay the groundwork for new ways of competing by developing and implementing a consumer direct pilot program.
4. Develop the market intelligence systems and processes needed to be a market leader in both targeted product development and service delivery.

1. Differentiate our service to our MortgageForce members via relationship management and MortgageForce PLUS. One of the key factors that led to our share gain in the past was our ability to deliver clearly superior service to the intermediary channel. Today our service superiority has diminished. A critical priority is to recreate and renew our service advantage. Two strategies will allow us to do so: (1) develop a stronger relationship management approach to the MortgageForce business and (2) fully implement MortgageForce PLUS.

Relationship management is a two-way, interactive process that starts with the sales force to create and nurture an ongoing relationship with our customers. As we look to the years ahead, the role of the sales force has never been more critical. In the face of heightened competition and the proliferation of MortgageForce look-alike programs, our salespeople are central to our efforts to differentiate Financorp from other lenders.

But relationship management is not just a sales responsibility. It involves other parts of the organization that interact with our MortgageForce members and customers, such as sales, marketing, operations and credit, and every part of the organization that supports these functions in serving our customers.

Another means of creating a strong service advantage lies in MortgageForce PLUS. Our customers have told us that this system's 30-minute on-line commitment provides a service advantage currently unmatched in the marketplace. Of importance, this system may provide us a sustainable advantage as none of our competitors will be able to match MortgageForce PLUS performance for three or more years. Therefore, we want to continue to push ahead in making this system available to our entire MortgageForce member base within nine months.

2. Create targeted products and marketing programs aimed at key consumer segments. Our examination of the consumer market reveals two groups of key interest: (1) first-time home buyers and (2) the affluent market. First-time home buyers provide us the opportunity to start a relationship that can lead to substantial cross-sell opportunities. The affluent market also represents a strong market opportunity for us because customers have such a high incidence of purchase activity for primary residences, second homes and investment homes. Moreover, focus on this market will allow us to capitalize on Financorp's customer base and to dovetail with other affluent initiatives throughout our banking businesses.

3. Lay the groundwork for new ways of competing by developing and implementing a consumer-direct pilot program. As we look ahead, it is clear that our continued reliance on mortgage intermediaries leaves us vulnerable. As we have seen in the past, the indirect channel has gained tremendous power at our expense as the number of formal lender-intermediary programs has increased. Intermediaries can pick and choose from a number of programs, switching their business at a moment's notice. Furthermore, while intermediaries still account for a significant share of mortgage originations, experienced borrowers are more likely to select a mortgage via direct channels.

Figure 2.3   SPOT Analysis of Financorp Residential Mortgage Business

Strengths	Problems
• Size/leadership position • Service delivery • Distribution channel support • Experienced/committed staff (in sales, new mortgage acquisitions and support services) • Broad product offering • Profitablity/strong portfolio • Financorp customer base and name recognition • Financial resources available to invest in business	• Lack of differentiated offering (i.e., service, product, price) • Inability to react quickly to changing market needs • Transaction, not relationship, driven • Only moderate credit/risk appetite; increase in credit losses • High fees to MortgageForce members • Interest rates to customers generally above the average in the marketplace • Lack of information on consumer needs and behavior

Opportunities	Threats
• New MortgageForce PLUS product as a differentiator • Use alternative distribution channels • Building a sales culture to create best sales force in industry • Targeted programs, products (e.g., our affluent customer strategy) • Building strong relationship management process • Build a service culture	• Inability to differentiate service delivery • MortgageForce/Mortgage-Force PLUS clones • Soft market and economy • Long-term housing demand issues (deteriorating infrastructure and unaffordability for first-time home buyers) • Entrenchment in other strong commercial banks and insurance companies • Concern about long-term role of intermediaries. Will the role of the inter-mediaries remain strong or be eroded by direct-to-customer sales?

Because the number of experienced borrowers will increase as the population ages, we may be at the beginning of a long-term market shift away from the indirect channels.

While in the short term our priorities are to improve our relationships with the indirect channel, we cannot be so shortsighted as to ignore our vulnerability with this channel. We believe that one of our major underleveraged strengths lies in our huge customer base. Finding ways to cross sell mortgages or gain repeat business from our current mortgage customers represents an enormous opportunity.

4. Develop the market intelligence capabilities needed to be a market leader both in targeted product development and service delivery. One of the key factors that has hampered us in the past has been the lack of important management information regarding the consumer market, the service priorities and expectations of our distribution channels and our own performance in meeting channel and consumer needs. We plan to develop this market intelligence over the next 12 months.

The four strategic thrusts just described form the basis of our activities in the next year. As we look toward this year, we realize we are facing some profound challenges. But we have strengths that no one else has, namely, a strong, committed and experienced organization; established and ongoing relationships with our MortgageForce members; and a tradition of market leadership. Together these provide us a strong base upon which to grow and build our position as a market leader.

Thinking about a SPOT Analysis of Your Business

As suggested by the Financorp Residential Mortgage situation, conducting a SPOT analysis can help you to develop an understanding of your business's capabilities for pursuing various opportunities, overcoming problems and avoiding or minimizing threats. When you apply a capabilities analysis to a specific situation, you are assessing the feasibility that you and the venture can handle a particular possibility effectively. Referring again to Figure 2.2, where does your new venture now stand with respect to each point?

Organizing information into the four cells of the SPOT model is just the beginning. Use the SPOT information and analysis to develop a list of what you believe your venture can do. Distinguish what it can do now with what it can do in a few months given some additional actions on your part. Each "can do" that you identify is not necessarily something that you will do. "Will do's" depend on several additional factors, including the venture's goals and consumer wants. Can do's are things that your use of the SPOT analysis suggests are viable given the venture's strengths, the problems needing resolution and the opportunities and threats you have identified.

- What can we do now?
- What can we do later, if. . .?

The possibilities for the future are limited only by your analysis and creativity. The possibilities that you are willing to pursue are a much smaller set of ideas. It is hopefully one that reflects some of the analysis and thinking you did as you read chapter 1 and conducted an assessment of the business environment.

To stimulate your ideas, particularly as they relate to developing a useful SPOT analysis, we must examine alternative strategies for accomplishing rapid growth. We begin this process by examining Box III of the 4-Box Model in chapter 3.

- How much profit is there for an average customer from this group?

- Do these volume buyers have any distinct demographics, psychographics, attitudes or buying patterns?

- Which geographic markets do we want to serve?

- Which groups are likely to be more loyal than others?

- Which groups will provide good referrals?

- Which groups will be more apt to pay on time?

- Which groups already use the channels of distribution that we have arranged?

- Which groups already read or see the promotional activities we conduct?

- Which groups are easy to reach?

- Which groups, if reached, will actively listen?

- Which groups offer the venture a high cross-sell potential?

- Which groups are not being served well by our competitors?

- Which groups do not have easy access to substitute products?

- Which groups might do us some disservice if they buy or are observed using our product?

Developing a Target Market Grid

By answering the previous questions regarding possible target groups, you have begun the process of developing a target market grid (or matrix). All of the attributes that your new venture wants in its target customers, as

Figure 3.2 Target Marketing Grid

Selection Criteria for Choosing the Target Groups	Possible Target Groups						
	A	B	C	D	E	F	G
1.							
2.							
3.							
4.							
5.							
6.							

well as the attributes that it does not want, are *not* likely to be present in many people. For example, customers who are the venture's largest purchasers may also be the least likely to pay on time. Or those who refer your products to another person may only be limited users themselves.

You need to develop a grid that captures the attributes of each prospective target group. Along one axis of the grid, list the prospective target groups (shown as A, B, C, etc. in Figure 3.2); along the other axis, list the selection criteria the venture wants to use to select the target groups (shown as 1, 2, 3, etc., in Figure 3.2).

The previous questions also can act as selection criteria for picking target groups (e.g., who are apt to be the large-volume buyers?). These criteria reflect things that the venture wants, as well as the likely wants of the consumers.

Criteria might also reflect questions related to the venture's ability to provide the product or service. For example, customers who place orders that *cannot* be filled on time or at all—given the venture's current and projected capacity—may not be the target group to pursue initially. Does the venture want to frustrate such potential customers by not being able to fill their orders?

The various groups that your venture can target also need to be defined. What meaningful differences exist in groups of prospective customers? Groups may be based on geography or location, state or country, industry code or on demographics, such as age, gender, nationality, weight and so on.

Figure 3.3   Globalcorp Grid of Markets by Possible Selection Criteria

Selection Criteria	Arizona	Florida	Texas	Pennsylvania
Globalcorp current relative market position	Moderate	Moderate	Weak	Strong
Long-term opportunity	Moderate	Good	Good	Moderate
Savings as a percent of disposable income for middle- and upper-middle-income market	6%	14%	3%	6%
Average number of financial institutions used per household	6	9	5	4
Number of accounts per main bank	2.5	1.8	2.4	2.6
Globalcorp average number of checks written per year per household on main bank checking account	182	148	136	124
Globalcorp average number of bounced checks per account per year	1.1	.4	1.9	1.5
Globalcorp credit card write-offs as percent of average net receivables	5.4	4.4	5.8	4.3

The growth challenge is to identify possible target groups that reflect meaningful differences in the selection criteria that are most germane to the profit and loss dynamics of the venture. Once a grid is created, you can develop a profitability model to identify the most profitable target groups as well as those target groups to which it may be easiest to sell (because the venture is able to satisfy more of their wants).

An Example: Globalcorp Target Marketing Grid.   An international financial and information services company, referred to as Globalcorp, was exploring the idea of starting or buying a banking-oriented business venture in several different states. They already conducted some business activities in each of the states that were being considered. They began their analysis of the market potential of different states by developing a grid of the various criteria that they viewed as bearing on their decision by the states that looked most promising. A portion of the grid is shown in Figure 3.3.

Each of the criteria had been selected because it related to what Global-corp had assessed a consumer might want or what it had linked to its profit-loss dynamics. Target market grids often start with a specification of what the business wants from the customer. To be effective, they must progress to attributes that capture what the consumer wants from the venture that the venture is capable of providing.

Overcome Barriers to Target Marketing

Targeting the venture's energies to the most profitable and probable consumers makes so much sense that one wonders why this advice is needed at all. Yet, two-thirds of the new venture managers queried on this issue indicated that they had drifted away from target marketing their preferred consumers as they began to grow. They indicated that their focus on the needs of their prime market was hampered by their desire to sell to anyone who wanted to buy.

In hindsight, these venture managers report that most of the consumers who were not in their target market talked a good game, and sounded like they wanted to buy, but they didn't buy. Terry, a partner in a new software company, put it this way: "People would call in because they saw some publicity on our new product. They would act very interested. We would send someone out to visit them with the hopes of a quick sale. Three to five sales calls later we still were selling, and they still were shopping. Most of the leads that came in through cold calls to us never generated a penny. People were shopping—and trying to learn from what we were doing without paying for it. We now screen people before we respond, and we get much more commitment up front before we send out a salesperson or a demo copy of our products."

The first barrier to overcome in target marketing is the desire not to deny the venture's product (or your time!) to anyone who inquires. *Target marketing involves denial.* If you are willing to dance with anyone who asks, be prepared to miss the opportunity to dance with the one with whom you really want to dance.

Denying someone does not mean overt rejection. Create a priority system—respond to those who meet your criteria first, and others after that. You may learn that the venture needs to add more criteria or change the criteria to reflect the market. That's fine. Denial is critical if the venture is to obtain rapid growth.

A second barrier to target marketing is the preparation that is required. It is not easy to identify the target groups, develop selection criteria and then collect the information to fill in the grid. Many new venture managers have explained, in great detail, why they had difficulty developing a grid. The groups they identified were new to the business, so there was no data on them or their behaviors. Some of the criteria they wanted to use to select groups was not available. To obtain the criteria, they would have had to do primary research or pay someone else to do the research. This would take time and money, which were not available.

The problems associated with developing a target market grid are many—the benefits of doing the thinking and analysis are worth the effort. Targeting does not guarantee rapid growth. It does allow the new venture to direct its energies, and those of its salespeople and marketing efforts, to the consumers who will help it grow rapidly. That is possible if the venture can reach the consumers with a message that clearly communicates the business's competitive advantage. As one new venture manager put it, without a targeting effort a venture is just "spitting into the wind."

POSITIONING

Positioning is a powerful tool of marketing that is frequently misunderstood. It is the *mental space* that consumers create in their minds for a product, service or institution. People who know of a firm or product will have some image of it. They will position it with whatever attributes they associate with the product relative to other substitute products of which they are aware. When the product is mentioned, or when they recall the product for some reason, this image comes to their minds. This image may or may *not* have the attributes desired by the venture's management. By exploring the examples and questions that follow, you may wish to alter the positioning of your new venture and its products in the minds of your targeted consumers.

Positioning Examples: 7-up, Avis, Citibank

7-up, which was in a low- to no-growth situation, developed a great positioning in the early 1980s to overcome this situation. They decided they wanted to be "the alternative to a cola." With this idea in mind, their advertising agency came up with a great slogan: "The Uncola."

The success of this slogan, along with heavy advertising expenditures to get the message to consumers, positioned 7-up as the one product for those who did not want to drink a cola beverage. The market share of 7-up nearly doubled in two years—truly rapid growth. By altering the way people thought of 7-up, the company positioned itself in a more desirable space in consumers' minds. Cola sales did not suffer from this positioning—other noncola beverages such as Dr. Pepper, Orange Crush and Canada Dry products took the beating.

Other firms have developed unique positioning slogans that have led to extensive growth. Avis pursued a "better service" positioning at a time when Hertz was getting sloppy with their service. Their slogan was "We try harder."

Citibank pursued a convenience positioning when they had more branches and automatic teller machines than many of their local competitors. Their slogan was "The Citi never sleeps." Deposits more than doubled during the period that Citibank had a convenience competitive advantage and "The Citi never sleeps" slogan. Neither of these factors exist today—competitive advantages do not last forever.

The Three Positioning Elements

These clever slogans capture a distinctive positioning, but positioning is more than slogans. Effective positioning involves the following three elements, which are part of the 4-Box Model:

1. Knowledge of your prime prospect and target market
2. A competitive frame
3. A meaningful point of difference

The *prime prospect and target market* includes the consumers who are considered the best potential purchasers of a product. Their purchases will contribute to both short-term and longer-term profits and business success.

The *competitive frame* refers to the customers' perceptual set—the group of products and services that customers will most likely consider as alternatives to the product. Alternative products include directly comparable products, substitute products and other products that satisfy the same customer need, although not necessarily the same want. Exceptional positioning hooks into the existing conceptual frame of the target customers in a different and distinctive way.

The *meaningful point of difference* is the specific consumer benefit that a venture wants customers to associate with its product. The meaningful point of difference needs to be

1. *important* to the customer;

2. *persuasive,* such that consumers believe it;

3. *deliverable*—in terms of the product being available and the point of difference being real to the consumer;

4. *unique* within the competitive frame (i.e., no other competitive product should have the same point of difference); and

5. *working against* the *broadest target market.*

Thinking about Your Positioning

As you contemplate your venture's products in the marketplace, consider the following questions to explore possible product positioning:

- How do our target consumers see our products?

- What do they think when our products are mentioned?

- How would our target consumers respond in two or three words to each of our products?

- What positioning do we want for our products?

- What do we want our target consumers to think about our products?

- What positioning do our key competitors have?

- How vulnerable is our positioning?

- Do we have the financial, manpower and product/service technology to sustain our positioning?

- Can our products truly match the desired positioning?

PRODUCT, PRICE, PLACE AND PROMOTION—THE FOUR P'S

The last areas of examination in Box III are the four P's: product, price, place and promotion. While these are frequently discussed as marketing tactics, they are much more to a new enterprise. The four P's (five P's if you include positioning) are the essence of a venture.

Product cannot be separated from technology, production, quality control, inventory, packaging and service.

Price is linked to production costs, product demand, sales, financial flows and image.

Place connects the product with buyers; it is part of an entire chain of distribution and is affected by the location of the plants or offices, raw materials and users.

Promotions are embellishments to the product such as packaging, merchandising and sales promotion activities. (Promotions may also include the various ways a venture communicates its products to consumers, including its advertising, personal selling efforts, direct-mail efforts, telemarketing and publicity. These latter aspects of promotion are treated separately in chapter 4 as part of the communications mix.)

By actively considering and resolving issues that relate to the four P's, you begin to lead a new venture, not just manage it. Are you leading it in the direction desired?

Product

Products (or services) have a host of features that the venture has designed into them. Every feature, including packaging, is intended to make a product more desirable to consumers and/or more cost-effective to produce and sell. As most advertising people say, features are *not* benefits. Just because a product has a particular feature does not mean that a consumer will decide to purchase the product because of that feature. *Consumers want benefits.*

Firms tend to design products with a variety of features. It is critical to think of products in terms of their benefits to those consumers who are the most probable customers. Without such a mental shift on your part, you will not relate to consumers in ways that stimulate rapid growth. You may love all of a product's features—customers only want its benefits. Write a book or instruction manual about your product's features; sell its benefits.

Product or Service. What does your venture offer—products or services? Of course, it may offer both, but is the customer really buying the product with some service added (e.g., a Swatch watch with a one-year service warrantee) or a service with some aspect of a product added (e.g., trend projection research provided in a written document)?

The difference between products and services is *not* trivial. Products tend to be things—they are tangible. As such, their manufacture can often be protected by patent or secrecy. They can generally be demonstrated at or before the point of sale. They can be examined prior to sale to ensure quality control; they can be inventoried and warehoused to smooth out erratic sales or fluctuations in demand.

Services involve doing something for someone. They are often described with action verbs (e.g., washing a car, providing a telecommunications service or transferring money from one party to another). When one provides a service, there are few tangible things for the customers to take away with them. The demonstration of the service often involves providing it in its entirety—at substantial cost of time and energy. As such, services may be easily copied by someone who experiences them without even paying for the demonstration.

Services tend to vary in quality depending on who is delivering them, and they are difficult to warehouse or store for future use. If a business has personnel available to provide a service, but it has few customers, it incurs much of the service expense without the sales revenue. With products, if a business produces too much, it places the finished goods in inventory. The cost of carrying inventory is generally much lower than the cost of employing service personnel who do not have a customer to serve. When inventory reaches unacceptable levels, it is possible to offer the product at a price discount or as part of a promotion to recoup some of its sunk costs.

The differences between products and services create varying challenges for attaining rapid growth. If a new venture is selling a product, rapid growth requires that it:

- Increase *production capacity* (or the availability of product) dramatically, generally through expansion of plant and equipment while slowly increasing its use of labor

- *Patent* or keep secret key aspects of the product's design and manufacture

- Use scientific methods for the purchase of raw materials, production scheduling and inventory control to ensure that the *quantity* and type of product are available when needed

- Create and apply a quantity-based statistical *quality control* system
- Handle *shipping* out of the plant(s) and warehouse(s) to key distribution outlets or end consumers
- *Train sales personnel* to demonstrate the product, take orders and call on distribution channel members
- Develop *monitoring and reward systems* to influence the performance of the production and sales personnel

If a new venture is selling a *service,* rapid growth requires that it:

- Define production capacity in terms of "who needs to do what to *deliver this service.*" (This typically involves increasing its use of labor dramatically, while minimizing its use of office space, plant and equipment.)
- *Service-mark* the service to protect its name
- Develop captive or proprietary *relationships* with outside service providers (e.g., franchises, partnerships, licensing agreements) to reduce the likelihood of others copying its ideas
- Define *service quality,* how it is to be measured and how it is to be monitored and rewarded
- Identify and *train customer service* personnel to both sell potential customers on the service and then deliver the service
- Develop effective *personnel scheduling* methods that respond to the preferences of customers, management and employees
- Ensure that trained customer service personnel are at the point of sale with the requisite knowledge to *demonstrate the service* that is offered
- Develop *monitoring and reward systems* to influence the performance of the sales and service personnel

By reflecting on these differences between product and service offerings, you can direct your attention to those aspects of the new venture that will demand the most attention for rapid growth to be achieved and sustained.

Thinking about Your Products.   New ventures need to explore new product possibilities, just as do mature businesses. However, their exploration of new products should be more restricted and targeted to the venture's competitive advantage and distinctive competence.

Consider the following questions with respect to your venture's product offering:

- Is a significant consumer or client want not being fully satisfied by existing products or the way the products are distributed?

- What voids or inefficiencies exist in the products offered, markets served or distribution systems used?

- What products would fill these voids?

- Is our product easily copied and delivered by competitors? How can the likelihood of this be reduced or delayed?

- Which product features are essential to product success?

- Can the most expensive attributes be optional and priced separately?

- How is product packaging contributing to the overall desirability of the product?

- What systems and staff are needed to support each product?

- Are there any product features that can be altered or eliminated to substantially cut production costs, operating systems demands and/or employee expenses?

- How might a preliminary new product offering differ from a full-scale rollout of a new product?

- How will each new product or enhanced product affect sales of our other products?

- What are the risks if we withdraw a product?

- Which managers are likely to be winners or losers if a new product succeeds? Fails?

- Are there people willing to champion a new product?

Place

Place, or channels of distribution, refers to the routes a venture uses to get its products or services to its customers. Some businesses sell directly to the consumer—they do not use retailers or wholesalers to move their products along. The most direct of these direct-to-the-customer businesses involves the manufacturer who sells directly from the plant to customers who visit the plant. Many cottage industries involve sales at the point of manufacture.

Direct response marketing activities, such as direct mail, telemarketing and personal selling, move the product from the manufacturer to the end user by way of a single medium—for example, the post office or other mail carrier, the phone lines or an internal sales force. The volume of unsolicited mail and sales phone calls we receive attests to the number of organizations that use these channels of distribution.

Indirect marketing is a term that was invented in the early 1970s to distinguish the traditional use of wholesalers, dealers, retailers and other middlemen from the direct response marketing channels just mentioned. Each middleman marks up the price of a product before transferring the product to the next link in the channel. In some industries, the markup may be 100 percent or more. For example, publishers sell books to bookstores that then sell them to consumers at about double the publisher's wholesale price. Book clubs often buy a book from a publisher for $5.00 and sell it for $20.00 or more. That is some markup.

Several channels of distribution can be used at the same time—placing additional demand on the venture's time and resources to manage the activities and relationships in each channel simultaneously. For each channel chosen, there will be some consumers who prefer to buy through that channel and others who have different preferences. Many people enjoy buying clothes and other home merchandise via direct-mail catalogs. Retail outlets may also carry these products, but consumers buy through the channel of their preference.

Thinking About Place. The choice of how to reach consumers in a venture's target market for each of its products requires careful attention to many factors. Consider the following questions as you reflect on your venture's products and their distribution channels:

- What is being distributed or acquired at the point of sale (e.g., the product itself, a promise of future delivery, an obligation to perform some service in the future, etc.)?

- What are our current channels of distribution?

- How effective is each in terms of total sales?

- Do different channels of distribution vary in quality of service and cost?

- What is the venture's profit margin for each channel of distribution?

- What value added, if any, does each intermediary contribute?

- What preferences do consumers or clients have for obtaining our products through some channels of distribution over others?

- Where is the product or service actually sold? Used?

- Might any difference in these points affect the choice of distribution channel?

- Is control over the product/service or customer important in the delivery of the product (e.g., service standards, credit approval)?

- Does the channel used affect the perceived product benefits?

- Do different target customers have different wants as a function of the channel they use for purchase?

- Do the channels used present the product in its most favorable light?

- Is the product merchandised well?

Price

Price is the value placed on something by the venture and its customers. Asking price is what is initially requested. If it is accepted, the venture has a sale, and the price of the product reflects the value that both the buyer and seller placed on the product. Otherwise, there is no sale. With no sale, the venture is left with an asking price but not a product's selling price. To achieve rapid growth, the selling price is the only price of relevance.

Price may vary in its level and structure. Price level (within any structure) is easy to discern. At my grocery store, apples are 50 cents a pound in the fall and a dollar a pound in the spring. Your grocery store may sell them by the unit: five apples for a dollar in the fall, three apples for a dollar in the spring. In both examples, there is a simple change in price level for the different seasons.

In comparing the price where I shop with where you shop, there is a change in *price structure*. Which apples are less expensive in the fall: those selling for 50 cents a pound or five for a dollar? Which are less expensive in the spring? One cannot determine this from the information given. Changing price structures has become a common way to make comparative price shopping difficult. It can be used by a new venture and its competitors to complicate or confound the real price being paid.

A number of industries have complex product pricing. Consider the typical home mortgage. The price of a mortgage involves an interest rate charged over the life of the loan (which can be variable or fixed), points charged at the closing (percentage points of the total loan to be paid at closing) and an application fee often charged by the lender as well. Is a 25-year fixed-rate mortgage on $100,000 at 9.0 percent with 3 points more or less expensive than a 20-year fixed-rate mortgage on $100,000 at 9.5 percent with 2 points? It takes a calculator and a few assumptions about the actual life of the mortgage to calculate the total price to maturity. The situation is even more complex if the comparison is between either of these mortgages and a 20-year variable-rate mortgage on $100,000 at 8.5 to 10.5 percent with 2 points. One must predict how the rate might vary over the life of the loan to determine its actual price.

The mortgage example suggests another key aspect of price: when does the consumer pay? At the point of sale? Over the lifetime of product use? For some fixed amount of time, independent of product use? Or as the consumer uses the product?

Xerox made a critical decision to lease their copiers during their rapid-growth years. This required more up-front capital to support production. Once this incremental capital was obtained, the decision served them well. They were able to maintain a stream of revenues from leased copiers that exceeded the sale price by a substantial amount. They provided copiers via lease that companies could *not* have afforded if they had to pay for them at the point of sale. Since the copiers were leased, Xerox offered a maintenance contract that "couldn't be refused." As copier technology advanced, or as the demand for copying exceeded the capabilities of the leased machine, Xerox was always on-site ready to lease the organization a better copier for only a small amount more per month than they were then paying.

Thinking about Price. In reflecting on the price of each of your venture's products, consider the following questions:

- What objectives is our business attempting to achieve via our product's price (e.g., market penetration and growth, market skimming, maximum profit margin, early cash recovery, satisfactory rate of return, product-line promotion)?

- On what do we base each of our product's prices?

- To what degree are consumers or clients sensitive to price level, price structure or changes in price?

- What are our costs?

- Are our costs substantially different than our leading competitors'?

- What is the relationship between our price and the value of the product to the customer?

- For similar products, is there a sufficient value difference to support price differentiation?

- If we consider a new price structure, how might consumers, the press, etc. react?

- What nonmonetary pricing factors are there in the purchase of our products (e.g., inconvenience, hassle, anxiety)?

———————————————————————————————

Promotion

Product promotions can mean many things—from merchandising to advertising. It is useful to distinguish between product promotion as embellishments to a product and product promotion as the communications necessary to sell a product. Promotion via a product's embellishments (packaging, merchandising and sales promotions) is discussed in the following three sections. Promotion via communications is discussed in chapter 4 as part of the communication mix (including advertising, personal selling, direct response marketing, publicity and internal communications).

Packaging.   Packaging for some products has become more important for sales than the product itself. Perfumes and cosmetics are often sold based on the look of the package or the color and shape of the bottle, with the contents being a secondary consideration for many buyers. Several new businesses have focused on packaging as the competitive advantage—for example, precooked microwave hamburgers. The packaging supports the convenience benefit. Avon Products introduces a series of new products each holiday season that leverage distinctive packaging as their competitive advantage. Catalog and direct-mail businesses, such as Harry and David, also use packaging to boost holiday sales.

What is the role of packaging for a new venture's products? If it is only to protect the product from dirt and breakage, the venture may be missing an opportunity to distinguish its product from the competition. Consider some of the packaging objectives identified by new venture managers:

- To protect the product from breakage beyond routine handling
- To reduce theft. (Compact discs are packaged much larger than necessary so as to reduce the ease of shoplifting in retail stores.)
- To reduce shipping volume or weight and thereby costs
- To reduce loss during shipping. (The post office has a minimum size for packages.)
- To attract attention at the point of sale—the goal of packaging for most businesses

- *Not* to attract attention during shipping. (Penthouse and other magazines package their products in gray plastic so as not to be noticed.)

- To create the impression that the consumer is getting more than the product's size would suggest. (Most computer software comes in big, book-sized containers even though the product is a small disk.)

- To provide the consumer with a package that can be used for other things (e.g., jams or nuts packaged in a glass or mug)

- To provide a reusable package (e.g., spray bottles that can be refilled)

- To signify a special occasion (holidays, graduations, anniversaries)

- To have the consumer feel special or feel that the product is special (jewelry boxes, packaging for some alcoholic beverages)

- For ease of transport. (Twelve-packs of beer have handles.)

- For ease of use (e.g., some microwave products, individually wrapped slices of cheese)

Packaging is as much a product benefit for many products as are the other product benefits that are listed on the package. Don't let your product's packaging be ignored. While one cannot judge a book by its cover, most consumers screen which books they pick up based on the book's cover before they make a purchase decision. This may not be an efficient or effective way for consumers to behave, but it is their behavior, nonetheless.

Merchandising. Merchandising is another aspect of promotion. How is a product displayed at the point of sale? How much space is provided for the product, and where is it displayed? Premier retailers, such as Bloomingdales, invest substantial energy and resources into merchandising some products well—and they let other products go begging for their sales locations, floor layouts and displays. Since all products cannot have the best floor location, lighting and physical arrangement, retailers choose which of their products will receive the most merchandising attention. If the new venture manager and sales personnel are not working closely with your retailers, substantial merchandising benefit may be lost.

The only way to control the way a product is merchandised is to influence the retail channel. Short of ownership of the retailer, many consumer-goods brand managers are able to influence retailers through frequent store visits and by providing special displays, trade promotions, cooperative advertising and salesperson good will. While a new venture may not control the merchandising decisions, it can know how its products are being handled and what it would take to have them merchandised more effectively.

Sales Promotions. Sales promotions are generally short-term events or activities that focus on increasing sales, brand loyalty and/or product use. A sales promotion is just one way a new venture can promote its products. Other ways include advertising, telemarketing, merchandising, direct mail, personal selling and publicity. The particular promotion methods used are likely to be most effective if they are designed to accomplish specific, measurable goals. This will be discussed further in chapter 4, which focuses on Box IV of the 4-Box Model.

New business ventures rarely have large marketing budgets to support extensive product promotions. The most common type of promotional activity is a sales promotion. Sales promotions include the following:

- *Providing refunds or rebates.* (Auto manufacturers are doing a lot of this.)
- *Sampling.* (Consumer package-goods firms do this with new soaps and cereals.)
- *Contests or sweepstakes.* (Book clubs frequently choose this method of sales promotion.)
- *Special events.* (Oil companies often sponsor special events.)
- *Continuity programs.* (The frequent flyer programs are continuity programs.)
- *Trade incentives.* (American Express uses trade incentives to get banks to push its traveler's checks.)
- *Value packs* (Bic and Gillette offer value packs in their disposable-product lines.)

The purpose of a sales promotion is to increase sales of a product during the promotion period—often a month or two. Sales promotions can help to close a sale, maintain current customers, increase product usage, increase the level or depth of a relationship, support and reinforce brand or product image advertising and generate distribution channel support.

Sales promotions *alone* cannot change consumer attitudes about a product, particularly if the attitudes are negative. Sales promotions can slow declining sales, but they rarely result in a product turnaround because a sales promotion does not generally overcome product or service problems. It is

Figure 3.4 Promotion Possibilities for Different Stakeholders

	Consumer	Trade	Sales Force
Sales presentations			
Speeches			
Demonstrations			
Premiums			
Contests			
Price specials			
Coupons			
Posters			
Point-of-sale displays			
Sales literature			
Catalogs			
Films			
Videos			
Packaging			
House publications			
Endorsements			

difficult to create a product or brand image with sales promotions because of their short duration. They cannot compensate for inadequate advertising.

Different sales promotions can encourage the behaviors of different people involved in the sale of a product. Using Figure 3.4, consider the sales promotion techniques for the end consumer, the trade (people in the distribution channel) and the venture's sales force. Which of these techniques is your venture currently using? What are you trying to accomplish with each sales promotion technique? With what success?

Thinking about Promotions. A new venture can embellish its products in a variety of ways. Consider the following questions as you reflect on the products you offer:

- What role does packaging play in the sale of our product?

- What other roles might packaging play, including becoming a benefit to the consumer?

- Is our packaging fulfilling the roles we have determined for it?

- How is our product displayed to the trade? To consumers? Does the front face front? Does it have its own display holder or case?

- Where is the product displayed?

- What other products are in the same area? Which products are contiguous?

- How does our product look among the competition at the point of sale? Better? Not noticed? Bigger? Cleaner? Lighter?

- What look do we want?

- What sales promotions do we use to stimulate sales?

- What trade promotions do we use to obtain more channel support?

- What sales-force promotions do we use to encourage and support the sales force?

Having considered many alternative strategies throughout this chapter, we now consider what is to be done and by whom. We explore these ideas along with an examination of the other elements of Box IV in chapter 4, "Promoting the Venture: People, Programs and Position."

4

Promoting the Venture: People, Programs and Position

The fourth box of the 4-Box Model focuses on the design and execution of activities and feedback systems. The thinking and analysis done to assess key aspects of the environment, analyze the current business situation and examine alternative strategies is the foundation for a new venture's future actions. Now decisions must be made regarding the mix of communications needed to effectively reach the venture's various audiences, the product programs to be communicated that will lead to accelerated sales growth and the monitoring systems and market research activities needed to track the success of the venture's efforts. (See Figure 4.1.)

COMMUNICATIONS MIX

Given a sense of the strategy and the competitive advantage you intend to communicate, who needs to hear about the venture and its products? Potential customers must be informed, as well as members of the distribution channels used. What about sales personnel, other employees and the media? To reach the relevant people with relevant messages, consider using several modes of communication: advertising, personal selling, direct response marketing, publicity and internal communications.

What percentage of your venture's marketing dollars will be committed to each mode? After careful evaluation, you will probably use some modes of communication more than others and will need to design specific messages for specific modes and media.

Figure 4.1   The 4-Box Model—Building the Business with Box IV

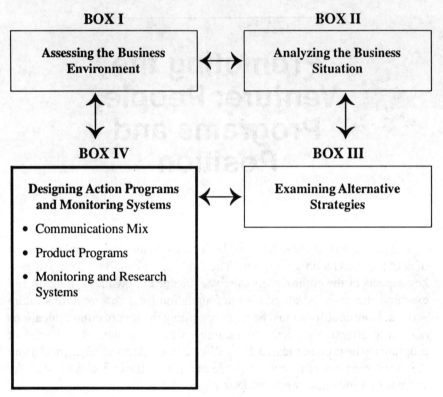

Advertising

Advertising activities range from putting a sign in the window to producing a 30-second television ad that is run on major national networks. The former may cost the venture less than $50; the latter could cost from $500,000 to $20 million. Given a new venture's business situation, national mass advertising, particularly by television, probably won't be viable for many products. But there are other types of advertising that can be cost-effective depending on the target market sought and the profit margin on each product.

Advertising works by creating awareness for a product. If a person is not aware that a product exists, he or she is an unlikely purchaser; at best, you might get impulse purchases at the cashier. Advertising also informs people and can generate interest in a product. It can remind people of a product and thereby increase the likelihood of purchase or repeat purchase.

Advertising adds perceptual value to a product if it is done well. (Think of the Coca-Cola and Pepsi ads.) It can also detract from a product if done poorly. (Think of the last ad that you disliked. Will you buy that product?) It may be better not to advertise than to do poor advertising.

Beth was the owner of a company that distributed a variety of specialty paper products to stationery and art supply stores for use with laser printers in desktop publishing activities. Having started the company three years earlier, she believed that the easy growth was over. Her venture had topped $1 million in sales for the first half of the year, but growth was slowing. She was exploring the idea of advertising to attract new business.

Conditions for Successful Advertising.   The first question to explore prior to a decision to advertise is whether or not the conditions are right for the venture to benefit much from advertising. Are the product and market conditions such that advertising dollars will result in the intended benefits? Advertising yields the biggest benefits when these conditions exist:

- Buyer awareness is low.
- Industry or product category sales are rising.
- The venture's competitive advantage is not easily observed by consumers.
- Opportunities for product differentiation are strong.
- Distribution channels can handle the projected increase in demand for the product.

If any of these conditions are not met, the return on the advertising dollars spent is diminished. Beth examined her desire to advertise against these preferred conditions. She concluded that buyer awareness was low, industry sales were rising, her competitive advantage was not easily observed by the distribution channels (although it was by the end consumers), product differentiation possibilities were strong and the distribution channels could support increased demand. The conditions seemed right; but should she advertise to end users or the trade channel, and what medium and message would be best?

Her decision ultimately came down to her preference for a push versus pull strategy. A push strategy would focus advertising on the distribution channel by getting them to push the product through the channel to the end customer. A pull strategy would focus on the end consumer. The goal was to have the end consumer ask for the product, thereby generating support in the distribution channel.

Beth decided to focus on the channel. End consumers knew what they wanted, and they didn't really care about the provider. Paper was paper—as long as it was colored and preprinted in desirable ways. Competition was still nonexistent in the markets Beth served.

Beth decided to run print ads in the trade press directed at stationery stores, art supply stores and desktop publishing supply outlets. She kept her ads simple, small in size and to the point. The message was that her enterprise provided quality white and color paper with preprinted patterns for use with laser printers and in desktop publishing activities.

Her orders doubled during the month following the ads. An investment of $11,070 in ad production and media resulted in an incremental $102,000 in orders. For about $7,000 per month, she could maintain the same level of media exposure. She decided to try it for six months. A year later she is still advertising, with near comparable results.

While advertising agencies and other ad advocates claim that ads can stimulate purchase behavior, increasing sales through advertising alone is a tough goal to accomplish. Beth's increase in sales came from the new orders of retail outlets with which she had not previously dealt. Consumer demand apparently existed for the product; her challenge was to get the product into the channels so that it could be purchased.

Well designed and executed advertising can generate consumer awareness and stimulate consumer interest in a product. If industry sales are rising, advertising efforts are more likely to reach an interested consumer. This will nudge the consumers' purchase process along toward desire for the product and ultimately its purchase. Whether or not consumers actually purchase your venture's product, or that of a competitor, depends on their remembering the product's competitive advantage and points of distinctiveness at the time they are ready—and able—to make a purchase. It also requires that the product be available where the consumer is inclined to shop for such products. Great advertising without distribution does wonders for the sales of competitor's products and substitute products. Beth was attuned to this as she made a quality advertising decision without much trial and error to guide her.

Given favorable conditions for advertising, consider the following questions:

- What have been your venture's experiences with different types and levels of advertising in the recent past?

- What levels and media are competitors using? With what success?

- What would happen if the competition advertised and you did not?

- To whom should you advertise? To the trade? To the consumer?

Advertising Goals. When a decision is made to advertise, the new venture manager needs to determine meaningful, measurable goals for the advertising effort. If you just want your product exposed, almost any advertising will suffice. If your venture is trying to generate substantial, favorable awareness and recall by people in the target market, it must determine the product's current awareness and recall levels. Moving consumer awareness in the target market from 50 to 80 percent will require a different type of ad than a goal to move awareness from 2 to 15 percent. Rather dramatic and frequently seen ads are needed to yield a big increase in awareness, particularly if there is only moderate product awareness today.

Awareness is the starting point. What is it in an ad that generates interest, desire for the product, conviction to purchase and finally purchase? If the goal is to increase *awareness* by 20 percent, consumer *interest* in the product will increase by less than 20 percent. (A 10 to 12 percent increase in interest would be considered excellent by most advertisers whose goal was an increase of 20 percent in awareness.) The goals for increasing desire, conviction and action would be proportionately less. By establishing goals for each step consumers take prior to actual purchase, you can evaluate the effectiveness of an advertising effort.

Advertising Messages and Media. Once advertising goals have been established, consider the kind of message and media that will help the venture reach these goals. The message should be tailored to the target market; its execution should focus on the consumer behaviors it is trying to influence most (e.g., awareness, interest, desire, conviction or purchase).

The choice of media should focus on the target market consumers— reaching them through a medium they regularly see at a time when they are receptive to the message. While most people think of television as the medium of choice, its cost and lack of focus make it a very inefficient medium to use. Radio permits more precise targeting of the audience and greater flexibility in the message communicated. Print media (newspapers, magazines, flyers, brochures, take-ones) allow advertisers to provide greater detail about their products, but print reaches a smaller number of target consumers than television or radio. Other media (e.g., billboards, transit advertising, ads in telephone booths, bus-stop shelter ads, etc.) can be very effective if they reach the target customer. Consumer recall of local poster media is higher per dollar spent than the other media alternatives.

Advertising Guidelines.   Once you decide to advertise, consider the following guidelines:

1. *KISS.* Keep it simple, stupid. The simpler the situation portrayed and the message sent, the higher the recall.

2. *Know the target market.* Restrict advertising to the target market consumer as much as is possible through the choice of media and message. If ads are reaching lots of people who are not in the target market, the venture is wasting its advertising dollars, or it needs to redefine its target market.

3. *Reinforce and remind.* Find a symbol, colors, patterns, graphics, a jingle or something else distinctive and stick with it. Kodak's packaging has never been great, but it is known everywhere. They have updated their packaging to be more contemporary, but it remains consistent with what it was. A new venture's goal is to brand its products. This involves continually reinforcing and reminding each customer at each point of sale that the venture's product is one thing and not something else. *Rapid growth demands a distinctive image;* reinforcing and reminding the customer via consistent advertising is one way to create such an image.

4. *Dramatize the message.* Have the message appeal to both the thoughts and feelings of the target consumer. The best messages appeal to all five senses—sight, hearing, smell, feelings and taste. Citibank's "The Citi never sleeps" message was much more dramatic than the "24-hour banking" and "The key to the Citi" messages under consideration at the time. "The Citi never sleeps" tag line remains the most frequently recalled tag line of all Citibank ads.

5. *Be distinctive.* Don't copy someone else's ad or message. Focus on your venture's competitive advantage and make the message unique. Find a way for your product to stand out from the advertising clutter of other products in a way that reflects its competitive advantage. People are exposed to 10,000 ads each day. American Tourister, for example, ran several ads focusing on the durability of their luggage. Unfortunately, durability was not a unique or distinctive competitive advantage for them in the minds of consumers. They advertised in a dramatic way. People recalled the ad, but not the sponsor. The sales of Samsonite went up, while American Tourister sales remained flat.

6. *Match the timing to purchase behavior.* Advertise when people are likely to be in the market. Give them what they want, when they want it (e.g., candy ads at Halloween or flower ads before Valentine's Day and Mother's Day). Know when people are in the market for your venture's products and start the ad campaign about one month earlier.

7. *Match the media with the message.* Leverage the strengths of the media used. Radio permits flexibility via the announcer—use it. Print ads permit greater detail about a product—share the key information. Billboards permit big, unusual scenes—go for it. Transit ads inside buses and subways get read word for word—make every word count including how to follow up and buy the product!

The potential benefits of advertising go beyond consumer awareness and moving consumers along in the purchase process. New venture managers who spend the most on advertising claimed the following additional benefits of their advertising efforts:

- "It helped move our products into the channel—the distributors were more willing to stock the product because of the advertising support."

- "The salespeople expressed greater confidence in our products, stayed with us longer and were more willing to stick with a prospect until a sale was made."

- "Our sales promotions did better when we ran some local newspaper advertisements at the same time."

- "The ads made a big difference in reaching some new customers—people we would not have known about or been able to reach had it not been for the radio ad."

- "The staff got very excited when they saw our first ads. They were charged up and ready to sell and service new customers."

Personal Selling

New venture managers have been doing this for years. They either sell an idea, their firm, a product or themselves—but selling is a major part of any new venture's success. The role of personal selling in the communications mix for a venture may be somewhat different than the personal selling done by new venture managers. For rapid growth, many people must become part of the sales process. But these people may not have the same role. What is the salesperson's primary role in the venture? As suggested in Figure 4.2, consider the different sales roles for your venture, along with how many people should be performing each role and whether or not the same person can perform multiple roles.

While most sales personnel can perform several of the roles and activities mentioned in Figure 4.2, few can perform all of them consistently well. What is most important to your venture right now? Are the salespeople trained for and informed of their roles? Is the sales force organized around regions, products, customers or some combination of these factors in a manner consistent with the salespersons' roles? And most importantly, are the venture's motivation and evaluation systems likely to direct people to the goals the venture wants to achieve?

Personal selling is the most frequently used form of communication, and it accounted for over 63 percent of the marketing budgets of the new business ventures that participated in this research. Many new venture managers wanted to do advertising but did not have sufficient funds to support a meaningful ad campaign. They invested their dollars in people rather than commercials or media. When asked "What lessons did you learn prior to achieving rapid growth that led you to make the changes necessary to achieve such growth?", the most common answer was "I learned how to build and lead a sales force—with specific goals, clear roles and responsibilities, quality training and compensation tied to performance." In Part III, "Thrust or Drift into the Next Decade?", we attend to these management, leadership and development issues directly.

Direct Response Marketing

Direct response marketing is a form of targeted selling whereby the venture makes direct contact with the consumer and provides a way for the

Figure 4.2 Alternative Roles for Sales Personnel

Role	Number of People and Skills Needed To Accomplish This Role
Deliver the product	
Build goodwill	
Educate prospects/consumers	
Solve customer problems before the sale	
Convey technical knowledge	
Prospect new customers	
Routinely sell existing customers	
Service existing customers	
Develop sales information systems	
Cross-sell other products	
Build account relationships	
Creatively sell new products	

consumer to respond. It is an interactive method of marketing that need not involve a salesperson.

Direct response marketing provides measurable results from each marketing effort, and it allows the venture to create a data base of responders and nonresponders for use in future efforts. Direct response methods include direct mail, telemarketing, computer networks, videotext and the use of direct response mechanisms in any media (e.g., print media clip-outs or postcards; poster, billboard, radio and television 800 or 900 telephone numbers).

Just as with a decision to advertise, a decision to use a direct response method requires that one know what the venture is trying to accomplish through the effort. Direct response marketing can help a new venture acquire new customers; consolidate, retain and cross-sell existing customers; generate leads and prospects; provide data for an information base; and notify and inform customers. What are you trying to accomplish through your venture's direct response marketing efforts?

Direct response is generally an *inefficient* way to generate awareness. An average direct-mail piece costs between $1.00 and $2.00 per unit. The average telemarketing call costs about $4.00 per answered call. Reaching 100,000 people with either of these methods is expensive; the return on this expense is likely to be low if the goal is primarily to generate awareness.

Direct response marketing methods are most successful when used against a highly targeted audience that is predisposed to do what the direct response solicitation is asking them to do. The response rates can vary from less than one-tenth of 1 percent (i.e., less than one response for every 1,000 contacts made) for a complex and/or expensive product with potentially wide consumer appeal (hence, it is difficult to target market) to 5 percent or more for a distinctive product offer to a clear target group.

The Response Rate Challenge.   The response rate is critical to the success of any direct response effort. These are some of the ways that new venture managers have been able to increase their response rates two- to threefold.

- Support direct response effort with a sales promotion. The direct response item made it to the best prospects; the sales promotion provides incremental inducement to buy now.

- Support direct response effort with advertising. Advertising was used to generate awareness so that when the direct response solicitation was received, it was more likely to receive attention.

- Support direct mail with telemarketing. This involved following up a direct-mail campaign with phone calls to ask for the sale.

- Use high-quality direct response mechanisms—direct mail, telemarketing or another means. The quality of the delivery system made a substantial difference in response rate.

Jacquie's Health Food Store.   Jacquie had opened a health food store in a college town, about half a mile from the main campus. She was working on a $700/month marketing budget. She placed fliers on campus bulletin boards and obtained some publicity in the college newspaper. The flier indicated that she was running a beginning-of-the-semester sale—everything was 10 percent off. She did no other advertising.

To stimulate sales, she decided to send the flier to the incoming freshman class (about 1,600 students). She obtained a mailing list from a friend who worked at the college. She mailed the flier to the list in September and waited for the response. According to her estimates, business increased about 15 percent during the two weeks following the mailing. She didn't think that the effort and expense of the mailing had been worth it.

I met Jacquie through a mutual friend. We started to talk about business, and she relayed her experience to me. After about 15 minutes of discussion, she agreed to take the following steps:

1. Remail the same list in three weeks.

2. Run an ad in the student newspaper to support the upcoming direct-mail effort. (This would cost about $100 per week.)

3. Use the same flier but indicate in a cover letter that she was making a special invitation to incoming students and that if they brought the letter to her store, she would take an additional 5 percent off their initial purchase (beyond the 10 percent sales promotion mentioned in the flier).

Jacquie estimated the total cost of the marketing effort to be about $800—just over her budget. If she could increase sales by 35 percent for one week, she would cover her incremental costs of doing the advertising and direct-mail effort. Sales increased 40 percent the first week, another 50 percent the second week and then remained essentially flat at that level (60 percent higher than the base period) until the next college vacation.

Jacquie now has a coordinated set of advertising, promotion and direct-mail activities that support each other. She changes the message each season to focus on different student groups. She has hired a store manager for her initial store and has opened a second store a mile away. Gross sales have increased from about $100,000 to nearly $1,000,000 within one year. Net profits remain about 18 percent of sales.

The Consulting Skills Workshop.   Another new venture had a different marketing challenge. A management consulting venture, The Learning Group, owned by Dale and Pat, was trying to generate business for its Consulting Skills Workshop. They had developed a list of prospects over a three-month period. Each prospect was a manager of computer system analysts in a midsized company.

The Consulting Skills Workshop that Dale and Pat developed was targeted to these managers; the workshop would train the participants on how to better provide systems consulting advice to the computer system end users within the firm. A letter and brochure had been sent to the 106 prospects that had been identified. A follow-up phone call to each prospect led to 11 sales calls. Three months later the 11 sales calls had led to two new clients.

While Dale and Pat were pleased with the new business, they felt that the marketing effort was too time-consuming. They asked, "What can we do to make it more efficient?" After some discussion, they decided to try again with their revised list of 122 names. In addition, they decided to take these steps:

1. Include a direct response mechanism with the cover letter. The direct response postcard asked the recipient to confirm the address of his or her business and to indicate the number of systems analysts he or she supervised.

2. Ask the addressee to circulate copies of the brochure (10 were provided) to his or her staff prior to a phone call either Dale or Pat would make to the manager in two weeks. The cover letter also asked the recipient to solicit input from his or her staff on the utility of the proposed Consulting Skills Workshop.

3. Make the phone calls two weeks later to coordinate a meeting to discuss the results of the recipient's survey of his or her employees regarding the proposed workshop.

Dale and Pat were not sure how many of the managers who received the letter and brochures would do as requested. They were pleased when 42 response cards were returned. They phoned all 122 people; 24 indicated that they had forgotten to send in the card but wanted to meet to discuss the Consulting Skills Workshop. Of the 42 that did respond, 34 agreed to a meeting. Of a possible 58 meetings, 43 actually took place. Eight of these firms are now using the Consulting Skills Workshop as part of their training of systems analysts.

These new venture stories are not unusual. People are growing their businesses rapidly each year, doing some of the same old stuff that you or I might consider no longer flashy or in vogue. With a good message to a well-targeted audience, traditional marketing can lead to exceptional results. But you have to do it. Thinking and talking about it are not enough.

Direct Response Marketing Guidelines. In each of the cases discussed, response rate was key. The number of direct-mail letters and follow-up phone calls that these ventures made created their expenses. Future revenues are a function of how many consumers or prospective clients respond in a way that leads to more profitable business. The Direct Marketing Association suggests the following ideas for boosting response rate:

•   *Know your audience.* Limit your distribution to the target market.

- *Eliminate the "turkeys" from the list.* Buy a purge list of people who do not want to be the targets of direct marketing, and eliminate chronic nonresponders and poor-quality customers from the list.

- *Use greed as a motivator.* Offer something extra to get a response.

- *Design your package* (sales pitch) so that it looks (sounds) like something people want—they often do.

- *Use involvement devices.* Get people touching, opening, writing on and scratching off something. Once they get involved, they are more likely to respond.

- *Keep the response device as easy as possible.* Don't make the customer write much or have to do much.

- *Question and answer formats work.* They tend to engage the prospect.

- *Personalize your method and message as much as possible.*

Jacquie increased her response rate by better knowing her audience (through more target mailings), using greed as a motivator (the extra 5 percent off) and personalizing her message (different messages for different student groups throughout the year). Dale and Pat knew their audience (managers of system analysts and the system analysts), used three involvement devices (the postcard, ten copies of the brochure to be circulated and a survey by the manager concerning the utility of a consulting skills workshop) and personalized their sales call based on the information collected in the follow-up phone call.

Common Mistakes in Direct Response Marketing. Doing direct response marketing the "right" way appears easy when you read about someone else's success. Yet, there are many mistakes made every day. Dennis Maginn, an entrepreneur and direct market specialist, notes the following common mistakes he has observed in direct response marketing:

- Not choosing your target wisely
- Not testing your offer
- Not personalizing your message
- Focusing on features instead of benefits
- Not having an offer
- Superficial copy

- Saving the best for last
- Poor follow-up
- Not asking for what you want
- Focusing on the product, not the prospect

As I was contemplating these common mistakes, I realized how easy it is to make them. They sounded a lot like the mistakes I made as a teenager during my courting years. Courting may be one of the most common direct response marketing efforts. How are we doing now?

Publicity

Publicity is any form of public display or communication relating to a venture, its management or its products that was not purchased. Publicity is not acquired or paid for in the same way as is advertising. Favorable publicity that praises, promotes or otherwise supports the activities of a new venture is what everyone wants. It is worth more to a new venture than an ad that was seen by the same people as saw the publicity because it was not paid for by the venture. People are more inclined to believe the independent reporting of the business press than a paid-for business advertisement.

Negative Publicity. Unfavorable publicity occurs when some of a venture's activities are criticized. The public is informed that a business, its management or its products are not as they seem or as the venture has stated them to be. Neither favorable nor unfavorable publicity is necessarily accurate. It is best thought of as the provider's point of view at one point in time.

It is often said that all publicity is good publicity. Publicity—favorable or unfavorable—helps create awareness. Against an awareness goal, all publicity provides a benefit. However, if publicity leads to disinterest or diminishes the desire for a new venture's products, it will work against the venture's growth goals.

Tylenol had substantial negative publicity several years ago when someone tampered with the product. The company, however, turned the unfavorable publicity into something positive by a very active advertising campaign showing how its product was improved and now tamper-resistant. The publicity itself generated awareness of the product, and this awareness stimulated a negative response: "Don't buy Tylenol." Through millions of dollars of advertising and addressing the packaging problem directly,

Tylenol made a great comeback. The company leveraged the publicity and turned a weakness into a strength.

Obtaining Publicity. There are many kinds of publicity. The most common is an article written in the local paper that mentions a new venture, its management or its products. Such publicity is rarely a random event. A reporter had an idea for a story and then went looking for facts to support it. If you are not available to the writer for an interview, someone else will be.

Getting publicity requires that you make yourself and information about your company available to the press and others who can promote (or harm) your new venture. If reporters, journalists and free-lance writers don't know much of interest about a new venture's situation, it will never get favorable publicity. It may even get negative publicity due to key managers avoiding the press.

There are other forms of publicity beyond media attention. When a venture's products, name, logo or other identifying symbol is displayed or exhibited, it is receiving publicity. When people wear t-shirts that have product information on them, they are providing publicity for that product. This is why Joe's Bar and Grill sponsors the local bowling team and corporations sponsor telethons, charities and other goodwill activities. By getting their name in front of the public by means of a favorable association to a charity, they hope to generate or maintain a positive image.

Obtaining favorable publicity contributes greatly to achieving rapid growth. Such publicity must be obtained repeatedly in key media and at desirable locations. As you reflect on how to obtain publicity for your venture and its activities (including hiring a publicist), consider the following questions:

- Is it necessary for the public to have a favorable impression of our venture or its products for the venture to attract or retain customers?

- What commercially significant newsworthy events take place in our market area? Can we (or the staff) get involved in these events?

- What role can our firm play, or what contributions can it make to community events, to derive favorable publicity?

- What role can we play in the community to support public activities and the social good? Which of these get regular media attention?

───

Internal Communications

When a business is small, internal communication means talking to yourself, sharing ideas with your partners and keeping a few key employees informed. As the venture expands, you try to keep up by personally sharing information with the relevant people as part of day-to-day activities. As you may have experienced, this soon becomes difficult, hit-and-miss and burdensome. New venture managers do not have the time for frequent informal communications with many co-workers, nor do they remember what they have communicated to whom.

Just as you have thought through questions regarding your new venture's advertising efforts—namely, who are the target customers, what do they need to know, how is the venture going to communicate with them and what is the specific message—you need to identify the target groups, messages and media for internal communications. Consider the following questions:

───

- What audiences need to be reached with what messages?

- Who are the key target groups that must be informed (subordinates, suppliers, the sales force, production workers, customer service representatives)?

- How often does information need to be provided (repeated) and updated?

- What channels should be used to carry or deliver the messages (e.g., in person, by memo, by electronic mail, by voice mail, at staff meetings, by newsletter, through the publicity received or advertising conducted)?

- Who should be the sender of the messages?

- What is the desired effect on the receiver of a message (awareness, attention, interest, information, initial evaluation, appreciation, desire, conviction, trial/purchase, evaluation, maintain/adopt/frequent use)?

- Does the communication intend to be casual, informational and/or persuasive?

- Is it likely to be perceived the way it was intended?

- If the intent is persuasion, what form of persuasion is most suitable to the situation (e.g., a speaker addressing an audience, an institution seeking support for a cause, inducements, threats)?

These are the questions raised by new venture managers after they have one or more ill-fated events within their organizations. Otherwise useful ideas or activities failed because of poor internal communications with key people.

PRODUCT PROGRAMS

Product programs are the various activities that are intended to get the venture's current and future products in front of and to the end users. Some people call product programs the tactics of business. Tactics are the devices new venture managers use to accomplish their strategies. Product programs are the detailed and structured elements of a new venture that help it accomplish its strategy and realize its vision. Product programs involve plans concerning who is to do what, by when, how and with what expected results. Action plans are often formulated around product programs to detail these who's, what's, when's and how's. The launch of a new product by the Levi Strauss Company provides an interesting example of many product program elements. Small business owners should also be asking the same questions about their products and services.

Tailored Classics at Levi

A new product development team at Levi Strauss launched a product line in the early 1980s called Tailored Classics. Tailored Classics was a moderate-priced line of menswear that was made of wool and wool blends. The product line included pants, sport coats and suit separates in a host of conservative patterns and colors. This was a new product line for Levi, as they had not previously produced or marketed clothes of this style, quality and material to a status-conscious customer. Their closest competitor, Haggar's Imperial Separates menswear line, focused on the more casual dresser who needed a suit for special occasions.

Levi started this product program by asking such questions as "Do new products or product lines need to be developed?" and "Do our products need to be altered to reflect changes in consumer tastes and preferences?" The stimulus for these questions came from a rather noticeable slowing in the growth of their jeans product lines and from the increased competition in the jeans market (e.g., designer jeans). The corporation embarked on this new venture to increase Levi sales, increase its profits and extend the Levi Strauss name into a new market segment.

Research was conducted by surveying hundreds of men on their clothing and shopping preferences. A segment of this menswear market, one that Levi came to label Classic Independents, appeared to be a large, under-served market. The classic independent male was characterized by Levi research as someone who liked to shop, who shopped alone, who knew what he liked and who went to specialty stores to buy it. The classic independent favored conservative clothes made of wool and wool blends. They were estimated to make up 21 percent of the menswear market and to purchase 46 percent of the wool and wool-blend products.

The initial segmentation research was promising, as it identified the classic independent male as a viable market segment to pursue. Work began on developing a line of clothes that would appeal to this segment. The Tailored Classics team was formed to lead Levi in this new venture. They began to plan their activities by asking and developing answers to the following types of questions:

1. *How long will it take to design and market test each new product?*

    One to two years is the typical answer in this industry. Levi needed to design a new fall clothing line in the late summer. Samples would be created in the fall and then ordered by retail store buyers in the late fall and early winter for ultimate delivery to the stores the next summer for the following fall's new line. If market testing is part of the prelaunch effort, it may require two full years to plan for and execute a new product line.

2. *Have we established a time line of activities and functions with respon-sibilities assigned and key delivery dates identified?*

   Such a time line was created with milestones to identify the key activities and decisions. It was reviewed regularly; adjustments were common as more information and ideas became available.

3. *Have budget issues been identified, and will funding be available when needed?*

   While funding for the initial research and product line development was ample, Levi failed to fund a market test, overlooked several con-sumer behavior issues prior to and during the product launch and never did the major advertising campaign it had planned. Obtaining funding subsequently became an ongoing issue for the Tailored Classics team.

4. *Which channels of distribution will be used? What training or informa-tion should be provided to dealers, agents, merchants, etc.?*

   Levi chose to distribute the Tailored Classics line in quality depart-ment stores—for volume sales, they said. Department store buyers were hesitant to stock the full line and perceived the line to be priced higher than the consumer would support. The classic independent male tended to shop in specialty stores and was not particularly price-sensitive.

   Levi chose a distribution channel that did not reflect the wants of the customers because it was convenient and cost-effective for them. The department store buyers did not stock the volumes of Tailored Classics Levi had expected because the buyers had misperceived the target customer's price sensitivity. They had, however, correctly assessed their typical shopper's price points. The choice of distribution channel and the pulling back of promised advertising and research funds resulted in a weak sales performance.

5. *What promotional methods will we use (e.g., sales promotions, mer-chandising, trade promotions)? How long will it take to develop the promotional materials? How long should the promotional period last? What are the projected results? What can be done during the promotion if the projected results do not occur?*

   The Tailored Classics team failed to consider promotions as part of their new product launch. They did lower the price of the product line to stimulate department store buyers to place orders, but this was not a trade or consumer promotion; it was a price change. Department store buyers might have been receptive to a trade promotion, as the economy was in a mild recession. Co-op advertising, sales discounts and perks for the store buyers might have helped obtain the channel support that never materialized.

6. *What staff and sales training is necessary to launch our new product and support our growth strategy? How long will it take to design and conduct the training? How should salespeople be motivated and compensated?*

   The Tailored Classics team was aware of the challenges in the sales training area. They hired a separate sales force to handle Tailored Classics and conducted the necessary sales training well in advance of the selling season. Compensation was based primarily on commissions—which turned out to be more risky than was first thought when the line was not actively bought by department store buyers. Within a few months, several of the sales people had quit; turnover exceeded 50 percent before the line had lived through a full season.

7. *Is it important to communicate aspects of our strategy and products to internal personnel and/or the public at large? When should this occur?*

   Both internal and public communications of the new line were critical to the success of Tailored Classics. Internal communications were frequent and effective during the prelaunch period. However, after the launch, communications to the internal stakeholders became noticeably less frequent. When sales did not materialize, the attitude shifted to one of blame rather than renewal and growth. Communications to consumers and the trade were planned but never executed. An ad was run in the Sunday *New York Times* to announce the line to the trade. Substantial consumer advertising by way of television or radio was not done.

8. *Have we communicated a control and review procedure to all those involved in the program with agreed-upon dates for reporting program status and progress?*

   While control and review procedures existed at Levi, they were systems based on Levi's past product successes with jeans. The procedures did not reflect the kinds of early indicators of success, or trouble, that start-up activities must have in order to adjust quickly to changes in the market or new understandings of the market by the new venture managers. For example, the focus group research that Levi undertook indicated that the use of the Levi name for products such as the Tailored Classics line was problematic. Levi was associated with casual wear. Would the name recognition and image of Levi jeans contribute to the sales of Tailored Classics? Consumers said it would not. Levi ignored this information and launched the product under the Levi name. More importantly, the company did not test market the product to see if the focus-group consumer concerns were widely held by their target customers, nor did they monitor the perception of the Tailored Classics line or the Levi name image to see if it was changing.

While it is easy to be critical of someone else's efforts, Levi's strategy for the Tailored Classics line was not ideal. The company's tactics and product programs were flawed in ways that could have been corrected had they applied a framework that encouraged them to review their activities as they proceeded. They did not adjust their product programs to reflect emerging information that was clearly contradictory to what they had planned. They needed to use and listen to their monitoring and research systems to a much greater extent than they did. (This is the final topic of Box IV.)

MONITORING AND RESEARCH SYSTEMS

The systems a new venture uses to monitor sales growth and profitability or to understand consumer wants and competitor activities are only a small portion of the monitoring and research efforts needed to create and sustain rapid growth. Every new venture manager interviewed monitored some aspects of performance and had a few ways of assessing consumer wants and competitor strengths and weaknesses. Few were satisfied with the systems they had in place. Many were doing little to alter the situation because they were either too busy or did not know what else to monitor or research.

A quick audit of your venture's current monitoring and research activities is a place to start.

- How do we measure success? Quality? Quality service?

- How do we know if acceptable profits are being made by a product? Region? Market segment? Trade channel?

- Are sales goals being achieved each month? Market share goals? Profit goals? Sales-to-expense ratio goals? Consumer awareness goals? Consumer interest goals? Consumer intent-to-purchase goals?

- Are the behaviors we are trying to influence in consumers, sales-people, distributors and others being monitored?

- What standards have we established to signify excellent, average and below-average performance?

- How does our performance compare to that of competitors?

As suggested by these questions, there are hundreds of behaviors and activities to monitor, and an even larger number of questions that can be researched. It is not the amount of monitoring or volume of research that is important but that you *monitor and research key aspects* of the business so you can lead it more effectively. Do you currently believe that your energies are directed toward the 20 percent of the business that leads to 80 percent of its profits? If your answer is an unqualified "yes," then you are probably monitoring and researching the most salient aspects of the venture (either formally or informally). If you are unsure of your answer or know that it is "no," then time needs to be devoted to exploring the answers to some questions on monitoring systems and market research.

SOME REFLECTIONS

Having read through dozens of ideas and an equal number of questions derived from the 4-Box Model, some reflection and a few observations may be useful. First, it is not possible to provide a new venture manager with simple answers, nor is it possible to provide new venture managers with a few guidelines to follow to achieve and sustain rapid growth. However, it is possible to provide you with extensive stimuli to "fill up your warehouse" with ideas and questions that can be accessed if needed.

Second, the 4-Box Model is not new (hopefully not, anyway). The ideas presented have been discussed by others—many times and in many ways. What is new is your effort to capture the highlights of managing a new venture on a single page, where the key elements are powerful enough to stimulate many thoughts and questions that you will carry with you and can access if needed. You are evolving a new mental model of your business that is more analytical and structured than the previous mental model that has developed from your experiences. Your previous model is still of great value as it is the framework from which your revised mental model evolves.

Third, the interconnectedness of the elements and boxes in the 4-Box Model is becoming apparent. It is difficult to talk about a pricing decision without understanding the venture's profit and loss dynamics, financial and marketing goals, competitor pricing, consumer wants, target market and so on. In fact, *the answers to the questions one can ask regarding any of the elements in the model might well reflect all of the other elements.*

Finally, we are not asking you to develop a business plan. You could do this, and it might be required by some lending sources or investors. Yet, it is not essential to have a business plan *documented* to achieve and sustain rapid growth. Roughly half of the new venture managers I have met have a business plan that they can show me. The others have piecemeal plans—some have no documented plan at all. What the most successful new venture managers have goes beyond their analysis—it includes their vision, passion, intuition and more. It is to these topics that we now turn.

Part Two

——————————————

Building the Business

Substantial business activity coupled with a growing number of opportunities to expand the product lines and distribution channels is both stimulating and overwhelming for most new venture managers. The excitement of success leads to a can-do attitude—and the corresponding belief that one can be successful in whatever direction one chooses to move the business. This can-do attitude is a wonderful motivator. It leads a new venture manager to try things that otherwise would not have been considered. It can also lead to devoting energy and attention to activities that do not lead to profitability or rapid growth.

Nelson, a successful leader of several new ventures, recalled one of his early failures. "We started out as a distributor of housewares. It was tough to get the first contract, but after that it was easier. Within six months we were distributing four lines of quality housewares, and several also-ran lines.

"We wanted more business, so we decided to put together a direct-mail catalog of the goods we distributed. We knew nothing about the direct-mail business, but thought that it would be similar to our distribution business, except with smaller shipments.

"A few months later," Nelson continued, "one of our suppliers was going out of business—so we bought his entire line. Without knowing it, we entered the discount sales business because that is the only way we could get the products to move fast enough. Before long, our profit margin began to shrink.

"By the end of the following year, we had a serious cash flow problem. We would have had to close within six months if things did not change. Fortunately, we managed to sell the business before the problems became worse.

"In hindsight, we had entered three businesses before we had excelled at our first business. We made a few bucks, but nowhere near as much as we might have made had we focused all of our energy on our initial business."

Direction is needed to channel a venture's energy. New venture managers need to focus on their venture's destination as well as how to get there. They need to communicate the venture's direction to employees and customers and must create an organizational culture that supports the way they want the venture to function. Chapter 5 examines how direction can be provided in each of these areas.

A second aspect of building the business, discussed in chapter 6, is understanding and developing stable relationships with the venture's stakeholders (i.e., the people and businesses that have a stake in the new venture and its products). Who are the new venture's stakeholders? Some stakeholders will be internal to the firm; others will be outside of the firm. Some will be very active; they may even tell you what they want from the business's activities. Other stakeholders will be more passive; they take what the venture offers—up to a point.

Once stakeholders are identified, their respective wants must be understood. Then the venture must determine if it can give them enough of what they want to have a productive and profitable relationship.

As a business grows, some new stakeholders need to be sought; for example, new suppliers may be required. The channels of distribution used may need to be expanded, and relationships with external support service providers (such as advertising agencies, public accounting firms or public relations firms) must be developed. If obtaining publicity can save thousands of advertising dollars, someone has to get the press interested in the venture's activities. The press should be made a stakeholder in the venture. As the number of employees and stakeholders increase, past relationships that had successfully developed get altered. For a venture to grow rapidly, stakeholder relationships must be managed.

Chapter 7 examines how the directions the new venture manager has suggested affect the various stakeholders. All stakeholders are not equally interested in the venture's destination, course of activities or culture. By examining which stakeholders are interested in different aspects of the business's activities, new venture managers are better able to provide the leadership and direction each stakeholder desires.

5

Direction, Direction, Direction

As a student in a continuing education course on buying real estate, I was asked, "What are the key factors that determine the salability of a property?" Before I could answer, someone shouted out, "location, location, location." To my initial surprise, this was the answer the instructor sought. It sounded dumb at first. But, as the instructor said, "one can buy bigger or smaller, change older for newer, remove partitions or add new walls, but you cannot change the location of the property nor have much influence on its environs beyond your property line." Location is key, and it clearly dominates all other factors that determine the marketability of a property.

Much like this principle in real estate, the top challenge for a new venture is direction, direction, direction. Direction is needed in many ways, three of which are quite distinct. Providing direction in one way, but not in the others, is inadequate. The three areas for direction are as follows:

1. *Direction as destination.* Sharing the venture's mission, vision and objectives.

2. *Direction as heading and course.* Identifying and following the venture's distinctive competence.

3. *Direction through management style.* Creating a shared sense of values and an organizational culture that supports rapid, profitable growth.

The aspect of leadership that new venture managers bring to a new venture—that is rarely provided by anyone else—is direction. New venture managers provide direction in many ways, quite possibly without distinguishing among these ways. As ventures become larger and more complex, it is critical to understand the different aspects of direction and to ensure that all aspects are attended to—if not by the new venture manager, by his or her most trusted employees.

Before reading on, *ask your people what direction you have been providing*. Depending on which people you ask, and their relationship to you and the venture, you will get answers much like those I have heard.

Direction as Destination

"You defined the purpose of our business."

"You presented us with a vision of what this business will become."

"You defined what it is that we want to achieve over the next five years."

"You established the objectives we must achieve each quarter."

"You set the sales goals."

"You determined the staffing levels."

Direction as Heading and Course

"You provided the product."

"You determined the kinds of products we offer and the markets we want to serve."

"You established the rules for what we can say about our products, as well as what we should not say."

"You determined the distribution channels and sales methods."

"You established the product's price."

"You provided guidelines for handling customer service inquiries and complaints."

"You determined the production schedule."

"You established the accounting and control systems."

"You approved major expenditures and capital budgeting projects."

Direction Through Management Style

"Your values guide our activities."

"You created a way of doing business."

"You encouraged teamwork."

"The supportive climate around here is what it is because of you."

Continuing to provide direction in these different ways is critical to achieving and sustaining rapid growth. Yet many new venture managers waffle in their direction after the venture's start-up period, just as Nelson did in the previous example. They take on activities that are really separate ventures in themselves while expecting employees to accommodate the increase in business complexity. They create ambiguity where clarity is wanted by employees.

This waffling may be the result of changing their destinations as new possibilities present themselves. Waffling may be due to a change in heading and course in response to various external forces. Or it may be the result of managers overlooking the importance of their managerial style on the emerging organizational culture.

The more successful new ventures —in terms of growth and profitability—do not waffle as much or for as long as the less successful new ventures. Direction is needed, wanted and desired in varying degrees and in different ways by the various people affected by the new venture. This does not imply that changes in direction are inappropriate but suggests that when changes in direction occur, they need to be widely communicated and accepted by those affected by the changes.

DIRECTION AS DESTINATION: SHARING THE VENTURE'S MISSION, VISION AND OBJECTIVES

Direction as destination is discussed under many labels, including mission, vision and objectives (or goals). The desire to grow a venture is an objective that affects many business decisions, just as the desire for more profits or a greater return on equity affect business decisions. Such objectives can be motivators in many organizations. But having a growth or profitability motivator is not the same as providing direction.

Growth and profit objectives are not likely to be met unless a broader sense of mission (reason for being) and vision (inspiration) are felt by both the new venture manager and each person involved in the new venture's activities.

What Is Your Reason for Being—What Is the Venture's Mission?

The venture's mission addresses the basic need for people to have a destination or outcome for their efforts. Why do people do what they are doing? Why are you doing what you are doing? If your answer is vague or slow in coming, take some time and thought to clarify it. Many ventures are launched based on someone's gut feeling that such a business activity is right, will be profitable and will satisfy consumer needs. Now that the venture is launched and has experienced initial success, this gut feeling needs to be communicated to others. A few people may intuitively know the venture's mission—particularly if they have been involved with it from the start. Most newcomers will not know its mission. It is time to articulate the mission in a few words: What is the venture's reason for being?

Examples of New Venture Missions. Paul Hawken writes of his mission when he founded Smith & Hawken: He wanted to recreate something that had been lost. In this case, he wanted to make available to the American market quality, English-style hand tools such as spades and forks. His motivation for this venture stemmed from a long-felt belief that American tools were poorly made, broke easily and had been accepted by consumers because higher-quality tools were not available.

Ben Cohen and Jerry Greenfield (Ben & Jerry's Ice Cream) decided to pursue their lifelong love of food in a business, so they decided to make the best ice cream available.

While these reasons for being may seem simple or trite, each mission provided clear direction to employees. Paul Hawken said, "Let's import some quality English merchandise for American gardeners." Ben and Jerry said, "Let's make the best ice cream possible and sell it to people who value food quality as much as we do." Both of these mission statements came from the heart of the new venture managers. No one was forcing them to create a venture. They followed their intuition and their sense of the market.

Not all new ventures are the inspiration of an entrepreneur. Many new venture managers are not entrepreneurs at all. They are family members or business managers who have sought out or now find themselves in the role of leader of a new venture. While their venture's mission may not be as ingrained and intuitive as it often is for an entrepreneur, it is still an essential aspect of direction.

One approach to developing a mission is to assess key market forces, trends and industry dynamics. This information can help you to articulate the venture's reason for being. A critical element in developing a mission statement is to define the industry or business areas in which the venture's products choose to compete.

Each industry has specific dimensions that define its being—often in terms of customers served, products offered, distribution channels used and technologies employed. You must develop a clear sense of the industry's structure along these dimensions in order to define your specific mission.

McDonald's fast-food restaurant did not define its business as providing all types of prepared foods—this would have been too broad. Nor did Paul Hawken define his mission to include the manufacture of quality hand tools, as this, too, would have been too broad. Smith & Hawken was established as a provider of quality English-style spades and forks. While this difference may appear small, for Smith & Hawken it was the difference between being a manufacturing company and an importer and direct-mail business.

Personalizing the Venture's Mission.   All too often the mission of one firm within an industry is articulated in the same way as the mission of other firms in the industry. This may be due to firms reading each other's mission statements, but I doubt it. I believe it is due to each firm trying to have its mission cover too much. These businesses want to be lots of things to lots of people. Such mission statements provide relatively little direction for the enterprise or its employees, but they permit the managers in these businesses to move the business in a variety of directions.

Ironically, less directional clarity often leads many to the same place because they read the same newspaper or collect comparable market research data. A phenomenon known as herding occurs—these firms tend to behave like each other, forming a herd that is predominantly moving in one direction. Over time, herding leads to an oversupply of goods and services in specific business areas and to the subsequent maturation and decline of many business enterprises within the industry. For a recent example, examine the first-mortgage market. Many financial institutions entered the area of residential real estate lending in the 1980s; today there is an oversupply of first-mortgage lenders, there are too many nonperforming loans and substantial red ink exists for many of the major players.

Articulating the Venture's Mission.   Developing an understanding of the venture's mission is a useful tool for building team spirit and defining a common agenda for the business. Involving more people from the business generally leads to greater awareness and acceptance of the venture's mission. Sharing the venture's mission with its primary stakeholders can also assist in energizing people to work toward the realization of the mission.

- What is the venture's mission, your reason for being? State it in ten words or less.

- Who should review the mission statement for clarity and accuracy before it is shared with all employees?

- How long do you think the mission statement will last before it is changed? If your horizon is less than ten years, consider revising the mission to be more lasting.

■ ——————————————————————————————————— ■

What Is Your Vision for the Venture?

A *vision* is a picture of the desired future state of the venture. It is often presented as a statement of what a new venture manager wants the business to look like at an unspecified future date. The mission provides fundamental direction and philosophy; the vision infuses the mission with value and inspires and helps translate the mission into an organizational reality.

Like metaphors in everyday language, vision statements have the ability to create a common understanding through the shaping powers of the images and symbols used in their articulation. For this reason, while a vision may be created by an individual, it is brought to life and creates a business reality when it is understood and shared by the members of the new venture.

Developing a Shared Vision.   A vision for a new venture can be useful for surfacing, recognizing and reconciling alternative and frequently competing beliefs about a venture's future state. Alan, a manager with whom we worked recently, had a vision for his unit that was different from the vision held by the majority of his newer staff. He saw his management development business as "creating quality experiential training tools for use in business and educational organizations."

Some of the newer staff saw the vision as "using quality experiential training tools to develop new relationships with prospective clients." The disparity between Alan and the staff had become apparent over a period of months as Alan took actions to move the business in the direction of sharing experiential training tools with other educators—at little or no fee to these educators. These activities did not contribute to the revenues of the business but did involve a greater number of people in the use of some new educational technologies. Alan believed that greater use of the tools in educational settings would lead to greater acceptance of them in business settings in the future.

After a series of meetings, Alan articulated the vision and developed momentum for enacting that vision from all but two of the organization's eight affiliates. The result was that substantial new commitments were made by Alan and the group to move in the direction defined by the now shared vision: "Share now, harvest later."

For some new venture managers, the process of conceptualizing a future state is easy; their challenge lies in creating acceptance for, and commitment to, the vision once it has been articulated. This can be facilitated by involving many of the venture's employees in the development of the vision and once developed, by communicating the vision to all employees.

For others, finding a vision is difficult. Some new venture managers ask their colleagues and partners to develop a vision for the business. Others ask friends to suggest a vision. Still others have looked for similarities and differences between their business and other businesses, with the goal of conceptualizing a vision from understanding these similarities and differences.

Fred Smith's vision for Federal Express came, in part, from comparing the possibility of an air express-mail business to bank clearinghouse activities. Fred Smith knew that it was impossible to ship packages overnight from city to city in the United States. By observing how checks are cleared in the banking industry by a central clearinghouse, he articulated his vision for Federal Express as an overnight express delivery service with a hub as the clearinghouse. The first Federal Express hub was built in Fred's hometown of Memphis.

Sharing the Venture's Vision.   The absence of a shared vision has profound consequences for new ventures. At the time that inspiration is most needed to stimulate growth, the lack of a clear, accepted vision is catastrophic. While established organizations can survive (and might even continue to prosper) with vague visions due to their momentum and excessive resources, the lack of a clear vision of where you want the venture to be in five to ten years undermines your ability to get there.

- What is your vision for the new venture? Your inspiration for being? Describe it in at least 50 words, symbols and/or pictures.

- Who should review the vision statement for clarity and impact before it is shared with all employees?

- How long do you think the vision will last? If your horizon is more than ten years, consider revising the vision to be more immediate.

Figure 5.1 One Bank U.S.—The Vision for a National Bank

- Draw the vision. Use whatever pictures, graphics, art, words and so forth that will make the vision come alive. You might reflect on the visions presented in Figures 5.1, 5.2 and 5.3 to stimulate your creativity.

If you have difficulty drawing a vision, tape-record a description of your vision for the venture. Give this to an artist or graphic illustrator. See what images it conjures up for others.

What Does the Venture Want To Accomplish—What Are Its Objectives and Goals?

While a great many things are important to the continuing operation of a new venture, objectives signify those activities that are most important for the venture over the current planning horizon—generally, six months to a year. Objectives can be identified by asking the question, "What are the key outcomes that will indicate our success during this year?"

Sometimes objectives are detailed in a business plan. At other times objectives emerge through the discussions new venture managers have with key staff members. "Improving customer service quality so as to distinguish

Figure 5.2   A Picture on the Wall at Jacquie's Health Food Store—Her Vision of Health, Nature and Accomplishment

ourselves as the best in our area" is an example of an objective of one new venture with which I have worked.

When a decision has to be made to allocate incremental resources to task A or task B, the venture's objectives should dictate which task to select. Responsibility for realizing objectives is not necessarily assigned to any one individual or subunit. Rather, objectives tend to be qualitative statements of the things the venture is trying to accomplish. Objectives are often a collective responsibility.

Goals are the specific outcomes that objectives are intended to achieve. They are generally quantitative statements that describe succinctly what is to be achieved, by whom and by when. Examples include "We want the mix of wholesale to retail business to move from 35 percent/65 percent to 25 percent/75 percent over the next 12 months," or "We plan introduce two new products into 80 percent of our distribution channels by the end of next quarter." The "we" in each of these statements is the business or a specific unit within the business; specific individuals are held accountable for the accomplishment of these goals.

The Venture's Objectives and Goals.   If the venture's mission and vision are clear and accepted, objectives can be created that are consistent with this mission and vision and that are flexible enough to permit people to accomplish a variety of things necessary to sustain profitability and growth.

Figure 5.3 The Management Consulting Group's Vision of Providing Clients with Stability and Insight

Management Consulting Group

- What are the venture's objectives? What are the primary things it wants to accomplish over the next 6 to 12 months?

- Identify two or three objectives for each of the following areas for each product (or group of products):
  Sales growth
  Market share
  Profitability
  Return on equity
  Number of distributors and/or retailers
  Production quality
  Inventory turn
  Customer service
  Collections and accounts receivable
  Management information needed
  Customer wants analysis
  Customer satisfaction analysis
  Employee staffing levels
  Employee satisfaction and morale

- Who should review these objectives for clarity and accuracy before they are shared with relevant employees?

- How long is the planning horizon for the venture's objectives? If the horizon is less than three months, consider revising some of the objectives to encompass a longer period of time. If it is more than a year, consider revising some of the objectives to be more immediate.

DIRECTION AS HEADING AND COURSE: IDENTIFYING AND FOLLOWING THE VENTURE'S DISTINCTIVE COMPETENCE

While the venture's mission, vision and objectives provide a sense of destination, you need to provide some guidance on how to get to this destination. People have joined you—as employees, customers, suppliers and distributors—because they find the destination proposed an exciting and a worthwhile place to go. They still need substantial guidance, encouragement and inspiration on how to get there from here.

As one proceeds on any journey, someone in the party generally suggests a course and heading—it may be a well thought-out course, or it may be determined as you go. The course may have been chosen with substantial thought as to scenery, travel time, traffic, enjoyment, lunch and a number of other desired trip attributes. Or the course may have been chosen to maximize one goal—the shortest travel time between two places.

People look to the new venture manager for a heading and course. This does not mean that all agree with the heading provided or that it will be the best heading. But some direction is better than no direction, and the new venture manager is at the helm.

Once a heading is established, people may ask questions about the course: What route will we take to get there from here? What stops will we make along the way? These questions may result in a change of heading to accomplish a goal that was not initially considered. *But at each point in time, the person at the helm is able to tell others what the heading is and what he or she hopes to accomplish by sustaining it.*

It is this type of heading—tracking toward a point on the horizon—that new venture managers must find within their ventures if they are going to sustain a heading during turbulent times. When the seas are fair and the sun is shining, most headings are easy to hold. But when conditions are turbulent and the sky is falling, it is difficult to know the moment-to-moment heading and is nearly impossible to hold the course. What is there in a new venture to provide this kind of direction during difficult times?

The venture's *distinctive competence* is a strong contender to provide the necessary direction to maintain a heading and stay the course. The strategy that has guided the venture during start-up probably encompasses its distinctive competence. However, it is the distinctive competence that is most important for the times ahead, not the strategy that encompassed it per se. *What is it about the venture that is uniquely yours and that is leading to the success you are experiencing?* This is the point on the horizon you use to maintain your bearing when the sea gets rough.

What is the venture's distinctive competence? It might be its competitive advantage. You probed for the venture's competitive advantage in chapter 3. But are you sure its competitive advantage is its distinctive competence? A competitive advantage is something that the venture can offer consumers that other firms have yet to offer. A competitive advantage at start-up may not be one now. Other firms may be providing the same service or product today or may introduce such products and services whenever they choose to do so.

A distinctive competence can be a competitive advantage, but competitive advantages do not need to leverage a venture's distinctive competencies. Building a profitable business requires the venture to understand and focus on its distinctive competence.

Before you commit to a distinctive competence as a guiding force for your venture's actions, consider some alternatives. A distinctive competence pulls the venture forward into the future. It is something deep within the venture, something that cannot be stolen or copied easily because it is an outgrowth of the early success of the business. No other business or new venture manager has had the same experiences as you have had in the start-up of this new venture. Its distinctive competency is intertwined with your knowledge and personality—thus, it is truly distinct.

It is difficult for outsiders to identify the distinctive competence of a business because they are not privy to all of the venture's past actions. Yet, observers can often detect a pattern of successful actions over time that are suggestive of a venture's distinctive competence. The ventures mentioned below seem to display such a pattern in their business activities. The pattern of activities suggests a distinctive competence that is being leveraged by the enterprise.

While it is possible for firms to have more than one guiding distinctive competence, most successful new ventures have a dominant competency that provides direction for its future activities. Using the 4-Box Model as a framework for thinking about different businesses, a variety of distinctive competencies are suggested. As you explore these examples and the distinctive competencies proposed, reflect on your venture's success. Why is it happening? Do your customers and employees agree?

Box I: Distinctive Competencies in the Business Environment

Ventures directed toward satisfying a particular set of consumer needs continually try to better serve the wants of their customers while trying to attract new customers that have similar wants. This is true of health food stores and many specialty shops (e.g., ethnic-food restaurants, The Body Shop, Bloomingdales). Some large enterprises also focus on satisfying the wants of specific consumer groups. (Examples of such enterprises are Merrill Lynch & Company and the Gillette Company.) By directing their energy, research and creativity to the specific consumer groups they wish to serve, these organizations have developed and sustained a competitive advantage.

Ventures directed toward excellence in customer service focus on the process of providing service. Service refers to someone or something doing something for someone. It is often intangible and cannot be warehoused or stored. Waitresses and waiters provide service to customers in terms of timely, error-free and competent handling of meals. Bank tellers and automated teller machines take deposits, disburse cash, transfer funds between accounts and answer inquiries. A number of firms have developed service as their distinctive competence and are pursuing it as their competitive advantage. Examples of such firms are McDonald's fast-food restaurants, Nordstrom department stores and Citibank Visa and MasterCard bank cards.

Ventures directed toward social or community responsibility focus on their values for a better environment in which to live. A substantial number of "green" businesses have emerged in the past decade. They focus on ecological needs such as recycling, pollution and emissions reduction and hydroponic foods. Planned Parenthood's initial focus on family responsibility has expanded to include social and community responsibilities.

Ventures directed through employee ownership focus on the betterment of the employee-owners. Employee ownership, in the form of stock ownership or a partnership legal arrangement, can become a firm's distinctive competence. For example, Avis advertises that customers should rent their cars from Avis owners—service people that own shares of the company. Partnerships often try to communicate that you should buy their service because the professional that handles your account is an owner, not just an employee. Many partnerships require partner approval for staffing decisions, new business development activities and line-of-business decisions. Television series that focus on partnerships (e.g., *L. A. Law)* often exemplify this process.

Ventures directed toward market niches focus their efforts on finding the next unfulfilled niche. The distinctive competence of a niche player is in the firm's ability to identify the gaps in markets. The soda, candy, tobacco and Lotto store that opens on a long, well-trafficked block that does not already have a store offering such products is a niche player. If several similar stores then open up, or other stores begin to stock the same products, the niche player may need to find another street. Korean green groceries in New York City function in just this way, as do many delis, gas stations and family restaurants.

Ventures directed toward trend leadership focus on identifying changes in consumer preferences. By identifying a trend earlier than competitors, a business can establish a market image as a trend leader. Firms such as Nike, Bennetton and The Limited have established such reputations. They are driven by the desire to be ahead of the pack. Some might argue that they create trends; careful following of these firms suggests that they do not. They identify a trend somewhere within their global industry and then deliver a product consistent with that trend in local markets.

Box II: Distinctive Competencies in the Business Situation

Ventures directed by business expertise focus on their core activities. Black & Decker did this with small power tools after World War II and extended its expertise into small appliances in the 1980s. The company has grown by leveraging its knowledge of home tools and small appliances— how to make them reliable, user-friendly and safe. This knowledge is built into each Black & Decker product.

Ventures directed by technology focus on leveraging their patents, copyrights and other proprietary information. Polaroid is an example of a well-known company that leveraged its technology for several decades.

Edwin Land continually worked to perfect instant photography, developing hundreds of patents in the process. Each new Polaroid product used these technological advances; new products were not introduced that did not capture Polaroid's distinctive technological competencies.

Ventures directed by production capacity focus on producing more of what they already produce. The Corning Glass company is an example of a firm that has a distinctive competence that reflects versatility in production capability. Corning produces hundreds of different products from a basic glass foundry. Specialized equipment has been added over the years to improve production quality and efficiency on select consumer items. Yet, Corning's direction—its pull into the future—continues to be based on its core business of producing quality glass products for household and industrial use.

Ventures directed toward the use of natural resources focus on finding and preserving those resources. The ski resorts in Vermont, Colorado or the Alps leverage their natural resources as their distinctive competence—in the winter for skiing, in the warm months for hiking. Different oil companies are examples of firms that use the same natural resource but have different distinctive competencies. Tenneco and Gulf Oil Corporation obtain their direction through the use and discovery of natural resources. In contrast, Exxon uses the profits from its natural resource businesses to pursue many other ventures—from office systems to retail convenience stores.

Box III: Distinctive Competencies in Alternative Strategies

Ventures directed toward market segments focus their energies on identifying new segments and then developing products and services to satisfy the wants of the consumers in those segments. By identifying consumer groups with different preferences for products and services, a business can tailor its offering, select the customers' preferred distribution channels and target communications to the wants of each consumer segment. Procter & Gamble, Unilever and Philip Morris are well known for their ability to identify market segments and then find ways to reach the specific target groups with distinctive preferences.

Market segmentation and targeting is also used for nonconsumer goods, such as industrial and commercial products. The General Electric Credit Corporation (GECC) targets large merchants of consumer goods for its credit programs. One of the private-label credit cards that you use may be under a service contract with GECC. For GECC to be profitable, it must identify the kinds of businesses that need consumer credit and customer loyalty to prosper.

Ventures directed toward a dominant positioning focus their energies on identifying new consumer wants and then developing products and services to satisfy those wants in all consumers. Some of the more pervasive wants of the past two decades have led several firms to pursue generic positioning. In the decaffeinated coffee business, there is Sanka; and in the area of sugar substitution, there is Nutrasweet. Pharmaceutical firms regularly pursue this strategy with prescription drugs and some of their over-the-counter drugs as well. They continually seek to discover a new product that becomes the generic solution to a type of illness.

Ventures directed toward products focus their energies on finding more users and new uses for their products. Using the existing product line as the source of direction is *not* a weakness. Knowing what the venture can offer during the early growth period, and offering it to all that might want it, can lead to economic growth and profitability. It is easy to criticize the large auto manufacturers and banks for their irresponsiveness, but they became large because they were guided by doing the same things for many people with great efficiencies. Their weakness is not in the leveraging of their earlier distinctive competence; it is in holding on to it as their driving force for decades after it had served its usefulness.

Ventures directed by their method of distribution focus their energies on creating relationships and efficiencies within the distribution channel. The telephone companies—AT&T, NYNEX, New England Telephone and others—use their lines and switching systems for most of their business. Their new services use the same delivery system (e.g., call waiting, call forwarding, touch-tone dialing). Their promotions and rate charges are intended to move telephone traffic to off-peak times—or to obtain premium pricing for usage at peak periods. Their distinctive competence is in the lines that connect everyone with everyone else. Their direction is to leverage these lines to the extent possible.

Ventures directed by price focus their energies on producing the highest-quality product possible at the lowest cost. If a business is pursuing a low-price strategy, it passes the benefits of low costs on to the consumer via the low product price. If a business is pursuing a high-price strategy, it invests some of the revenues associated with the high profit margin into building and sustaining a prestigious image. Some service industries are directed by low price—for example, discount brokerage firms. In contrast, high price is the direction taken by Rolls Royce cars and Joy perfumes.

While quality claims are made, the distinctiveness of the product is as much its high price as it is quality.

Ventures directed toward their method of sale focus their energies on perfecting that selling method. Avon Products, Inc. is most noted for its door-to-door method of sale. Avon representatives call on prospective customers in their neighborhoods, show the product line and deliver the products offered. Tupperware and Fuller brushes are distributed in this manner. It is interesting to observe that each of these firms uses additional channels of distribution today (e.g., direct-mail marketing activity and opening retail outlets).

Ventures directed toward sales promotions focus their energies on finding clever and noteworthy ways of offering their products at a discount. Comb Liquidators buys merchandise that a manufacturer no longer makes and sells it via direct-mail catalog at a discount. Comb promotes its products as quality products that are discontinued. Its target customer is the person who wants a product of reasonable quality, from a known manufacturer, at a big discount. By buying last year's model, colors and so forth, the customer gets a better price without sacrificing brand-name quality.

A different kind of promotion is used by Publishers Clearing House. They provide a sizable discount, but their promotions are not discounts per se. Publishers Clearing House conducts sweepstakes; consumers need only return the direct-mail form to be entered in the sweepstakes for a chance at winning something valuable (e.g., a car). While you need not purchase anything to enter the sweepstakes, many people find the sweepstakes promotion and the products to their liking.

Ventures directed toward merchandising focus their energies on creating a distinctive point-of-sale display or event. Many firms use merchandising as their distinctive competence—for example, the manufacturers of those candies, cigarettes and magazines by the checkout counter. The businesses behind these products often provide point-of-sale displays, product containers and racks to increase the likelihood that their products will be merchandised as they wish. L'eggs, Frookies, Duracell batteries, Kodak film and many other consumables are driven by their merchandising efforts.

Box IV: Program-Based Distinctive Competencies

Ventures directed toward creating and sustaining public awareness and a positive image focus their energies on communications with the public, including advertising and public affairs. Many sports teams have grown their franchises, increased attendance at games and sold millions of dollars worth of t-shirts, hats and other memorabilia based on their image. They sustain the image by having key players or the entire team support public welfare activities—for example, speaking out against drugs or encouraging young people to stay in school.

Ventures directed toward direct response marketing focus their energies on finding and reaching consumers in their target market. Smith & Hawken, a premier mail-order garden tool company, exemplifies a business that leverages its direct-mail distinctive competence. Smith & Hawken provides 24-hour turnaround for orders and provides money-back guarantees. By expanding the products offered in its catalog from quality hand tools to gardening supplies and horticulture products, Smith & Hawken has sustained rapid growth and profitability by servicing more of the needs of its target customers.

Ventures directed toward obtaining publicity and media support focus their energies on finding and involving themselves in mediaworthy events. Special interest groups—whether antinuclear or right-to-life—push their points of view through the media. Without media attention, most of these groups would not exist or succeed in altering public opinion. Their members must continually do things that obtain media attention—hopefully, positive attention. Yet, negative publicity often adds value to their causes.

Ventures directed by management information systems focus their energies on using business information to identify future opportunities. Many service ventures are in relationship businesses. A nursing-care new venture was created to provide temporary, home nursing care on a visiting, short-notice basis, much like temporary office help. People in need of a nurse would call the agency. The agency retained a staff of several dozen nurses and had a file on several hundred nurses available for day care, evening care and/or emergency care. Nurses were carefully screened, assigned to customers based on their skills and preferences and monitored/evaluated on 32 key behaviors after each day of work.

It is the information base that drives this temporary home-nursing business. The survival and growth of the business depends on the nurses being asked back for multiple-day assignments and referrals by customers. Payment forms must also be completed properly. The profitability of the business is linked closely to its growth, subject to the delivery of excellent health care. The firm has survived start-up and has grown several fold over three years. The new venture managers in charge of the venture both agree that their continued success is directly tied to their ability to monitor and evaluate their staff daily, while providing positive and constructive feedback to each visiting nurse at the end of his or her duty day.

Ventures directed toward market research focus their energies on collecting and packaging information. Accountline, a survey research firm specializing in the financial services industry, collects data from a random sample of consumers each month. It asks the consumers questions about their banking activities and then sells the information to financial institutions.

Thoughts about Your Heading and Course

Having explored possible distinctive competencies of several well-known businesses, as well as some new ventures, consider the following questions for your venture:

• What is the distinctive competence of the venture?

• Why is this distinctive?

• What is the competency that we are exhibiting?

• Does this distinctive competence provide the point on the horizon that can guide the business through tough times?

• How will it do this?

DIRECTION THROUGH MANAGEMENT STYLE: CREATING A SHARED SENSE OF VALUES AND AN ORGANIZATIONAL CULTURE THAT SUPPORTS RAPID, PROFITABLE GROWTH

People work for a new venture for many reasons—the novelty of doing new things, the excitement of starting up a business or the challenge of taking on the establishment. People work for a new venture because they hope to be part of its success and share in the financial rewards of that success. And many people claim that they work for a new venture because they do not want to work for big business. Whatever the reasons, people rarely state that they accepted a job in a new venture because their initial take-home pay was greater than what they could have made (or were making) by working for a large corporation or the government. It is not the short-term financial reward that draws people into new businesses. It is the excitement and intensity of new venture activities, as well as the opportunity to do things the way they believe is best.

The people who are most instrumental in helping new ventures to grow profitably have a number of things in common. First, they can articulate the new venture's mission and vision in terms that are consistent with the views of the founder and new venture manager. Second, they can identify the venture's distinctive competence and competitive advantage clearly—in nontechnical terms and with little or no hesitation. They know the areas where the venture excels. These people are clear on the venture's destination and the course it is taking to get there.

A third element is also common to successful new ventures. *The new venture managers and employees indicate the existence of a shared sense of values and a culture that meets their personal and professional needs.* By asking people what they saw as the shared values and culture, we identified a set of attributes common to many ventures. These 20 attributes are presented in Figure 5.4. No single venture was described by the entire list.

Most new ventures were characterized by the majority of their employees by eight to ten of these attributes. Those new ventures that had greater agreement on the shared values and culture had less turnover than new ventures that indicated little or no agreement on a set of values and culture. Hence, the third area where direction is needed is with respect to the values and culture of the enterprise. The new venture manager sets the tone; staffing decisions, venture policies and procedures reinforce the values espoused and build a culture to sustain them.

As you reflect on your values and the new venture culture that these values are creating, explore whether or not the venture is following these values. To do this, rate each item in Figure 5.4 on a scale from 0 to 100 percent by answering the question, "What percentage of our employees will state that this attribute is part of our culture?"

Having developed a personal sense of your venture's culture, have the venture's partners and other managers complete the same task. *Do you agree, as a management group, as to the key attributes of the venture's culture?* By identifying areas of agreement and disagreement, you are embarking on a process to establish the third type of direction: creating a management style that can reinforce espoused values and culture.

Figure 5.4 Attributes of Management Style

Management Style Attributes	Percent Agreement
1. People are supportive of the ideas of others.	
2. People are trustworthy and trusting of each other.	
3. People are oriented toward action and results.	
4. People are open to new or different ideas.	
5. People are cooperative and are team players.	
6. People are good listeners; they make others feel heard.	
7. People are conservative in their decisions and actions.	
8. People actively network and develop relationships with each other and with customers, buyers and suppliers.	
9. People are focused on priority issues.	
10. People share their goals openly and willingly.	
11. People are asked to participate in decision making.	
12. People are customer-service oriented.	
13. People thoroughly discuss conflicts and share differing points of view.	
14. People feel personally accountable for their contributions to the business.	
15. People see the culture as egalitarian; all are respected for their ideas.	
16. People are energetic and motivated.	
17. People strive for excellence in all they do.	
18. People support entrepreneurial behavior; they like to champion new things and perceive the rewards to be worth the risks.	
19. People actively seek control when unforeseen events happen.	
20. People feel committed to the organization; they do not intend to leave.	

It is possible to use the survey information in Figure 5.4 to clarify the values that are important. The next step is to understand how others perceive and experience the new venture's activities. To do this in a comprehensive way, another tool is needed. We need to understand the venture's various stakeholders, their wants and how they experience the venture.

6

Identifying and Understanding Stakeholders

Having established a sense of direction, it is critical to determine who needs to be informed of and accept this direction—in terms of destination, course and management style. Providing direction is a beginning. Direction can create a sense of personal comfort and inspiration for the challenges ahead. More importantly, having a mission and vision, a clear sense of the venture's distinctive competence and sharing values and a culture are valuable because of their effects on the significant others connected in some way with the new venture. These significant others will contribute to and manage the rapid growth you seek.

Who are the people who *touch* the new venture in direct and significant ways (e.g., customers, employees and sources of capital) or in indirect, more limited ways (e.g., neighbors, providers of supplies or the local assemblyman or councilwoman)? These *stakeholders* include individuals, groups and organizations that have a stake in what happens to the venture. They have many needs and wants of their own, some of which will have something to do with the new venture.

Stakeholders have some wants that translate into issues to which the venture must respond or attend. These stakeholder issues affect venture growth and profitability. The effective resolution of these issues will facilitate reaching the sweet spot and may very well determine just how sweet that sweet spot will be.

There are many people and businesses that touch a new venture—it is overwhelming to think about them all at once. What is needed is a framework for *identifying the key stakeholders* for issues related to the directions proposed by the venture. By knowing who the stakeholders are, the new venture manager can explore what it is they want from the venture and what the venture will offer them. To start our thinking about stakeholders, consider the following questions:

- Who are the venture's key stakeholders?

- What is their stake in the business activities?

- What do they need the venture for—is it the delivery of a product or service, continued employment, a financial or emotional return on their investments or as a customer for their business activities?

- What is the venture willing to offer them?

- Will this be enough to obtain their continued involvement?

- If not, what else might the venture offer that they want?

The answers to these questions lead to a detailed understanding of the influences that have emerged over the venture's start-up period. Since all influences on the venture can be linked to people and their decisions, knowing the venture's stakeholders is critical for continued success.

This approach to understanding who influences the venture's activities and decisions requires you to diagnose who the venture's stakeholders are by examining the various points of contact the venture has with those within the venture as well as people and institutions in the environment. Points of contact are easily identified by exploring the flows inherent in the venture: money flows, people flows, material flows and idea flows. Where does the venture obtain each type of resource, what happens to it next and so on until each transaction is completed and audited.

Once stakeholders are identified, new venture managers can examine what the stakeholders want from the venture, how they might influence those wants and which of those wants the venture might satisfy.

STAKEHOLDER ANALYSIS

A new venture has many stakeholders, and some stakeholders are more important to the venture's success than others. *Active stakeholders* are people and organizations that require the new venture to satisfy some of their wants in order to obtain their business or approval and/or to avoid their active resistance. *Passive stakeholders* influence a venture through their effect on the environment in which the venture exists (e.g., government regulators, technology providers) or through their reactions to the venture's business activities. Passive stakeholders may become active stakeholders if the situation changes such that their perceived stake in the new venture increases enough to warrant active involvement.

In addition to active and passive stakeholders, it is useful to distinguish between stakeholders that are external or internal to the venture. *External stakeholders* are people and organizations that do not directly or indirectly report to the head of the venture and that are outside of the venture's legal boundary. *Internal stakeholders* are the manager-owners and employees—part-time, full-time and voluntary.

Examples of stakeholders that reflect the active-passive and external-internal dimensions are listed in Figure 6.1. It is the active external and active internal stakeholders who have the greatest stake in the new venture's success, followed by the passive internal stakeholders and finally the passive external stakeholders. Because active stakeholders have a high stake in the venture, their behaviors and preferences should be monitored, and the useful information obtained should be incorporated into the venture's decisions.

Within each category of stakeholder, some of the stakeholders are likely to influence (or want to influence) the new venture's activities and decisions more than others. Those who tend to desire the greatest influence are listed at the top of each column, and the stakeholders lower in their desire to influence are listed further down in the column.

Active External Stakeholders

Active external stakeholders are the venture's customers, funding sources (other than partners), trade or distribution channel buyers, suppliers of goods and services and various other businesses affiliated with the venture through competition and arrangements such as joint ventures, trading partnerships, licenses, importers and exporters.

Figure 6.1   Stakeholders and Their Potential Influence on New Venture Activities and Decisions

Stake in Venture Success

High	High	Moderate	Low
Stakeholder Categories			
Active External Stakeholders	*Active Internal Stakeholders*	*Passive Internal Stakeholders*	*Passive External Stakeholders*
Customers	Partners	Staff workers	Regulators
Funding sources	Bosses (board of directors)	Labor force (if unskilled and not unionized)	Local governments
Trade and distribution channel buyers	Direct subordinates		Technology providers
Suppliers	Line employees		Journalists and venture analysts
Other businesses (e.g., competitors, joint ventures, trading partners, licensers, importers, exporters) ↓	Organized labor Contributed labor (e.g., voluntary help, family workers)		Consumer interest groups
Decreasing Influence on Venture Actions and Decisions			

Customers. Customers include those who buy or use the venture's products or services. It is useful to categorize the different types of customers so you can be more sensitive to their potentially different wants. Individual customers may be onetime buyers or repeat purchasers. Some customers are loyal; others are not. Some may purchase for their own consumption, others for their venture's activities and still others for gift giving. Individual buyers should be examined separately from venture buyers, educational buyers and wholesalers (people who buy with the intention to resell but who are not viewed by the new venture as formal channels of distribution). The wants of these different customers may vary substantially for some products and services. *The goal for the venture is to satisfy enough of the wants of each type of customer to obtain their continued patronage.*

Some businesses overlook the nonpurchasing customer as a stakeholder. If someone uses your product—whether or not the person purchases it, receives it as a gift or simply just uses it—he or she has a stake in the venture's continued success. That customer may need service, want to buy a replacement, provide product referrals and/or want more of the product to use in the future.

Magazine publishers and firms advertising in magazines know that many of the readers of magazines do not buy them. Some magazines, such as *Newsweek* and *People,* are circulated and made available in doctors' waiting rooms. Select magazines are provided for free use on most airlines. The Delta and U.S. Air shuttles give away copies of magazines to their customers (along with free coffee and newspapers). Many people who read these magazines and newspapers do not purchase them.

Customers, as a group, have a high stake in a new venture and want to influence the venture's actions and decisions quite strongly. As an individual, a customer's stake and influence is much smaller. *To grow the venture, maximize the customer's stake in it and permit customers as a group to have extensive influence.* This advice may seem counterintuitive at first. Why not minimize the number of different stakeholders, or minimize their influence, to make life easier? The answer is simple: Growth and profits do not come easily. As one new venture manager said, "If new venture managers wanted an easy life, they would work for someone else."

Funding Sources. The second active external stakeholder group is the venture's funding sources. These stakeholders include those responsible for the funding provided by banks and other financial institutions; venture capitalists; investors in stock, bonds and commercial paper; personal loan providers; and personal money lenders such as family members and friends. *As a general rule, the larger the stake and the more bureaucratic the funding provider, the greater its desire to control the venture's activities and decisions.*

To maintain control over the venture and to minimize the need of the venture to satisfy the wants of many funding sources, it is better to have borrowed small amounts from nonbureaucratic sources. Access to too much capital seems to make new venture managers foolish—they lose their ability to think critically and strategically. More promising new ventures have failed due to too much money rather than not enough. Not-so-promising new ventures fail independent of the funding situation.

To get the greatest *incremental* financial support during difficult times, it is better to have borrowed a large amount from a large, stable bank or financial institution. As Fred Smith, the founder and CEO of Federal Express, states, "If you borrow a little and have a problem, you have a creditor after you. If you borrow a lot and have a problem, you have a partner." In difficult times, new venture managers need partners in their financial activities. In good times, they need partnerships in their production, marketing and distribution activities. Be clear of your needs as a function of how well things are progressing. Remember, the bigger the financial institution, the more likely it will be to lend you money when you do not really need it. Be sure you need it.

Trade and Distribution Channel Buyers. Trade and distribution channel buyers are a third active external stakeholder group. The people and businesses that make up the venture's distribution channels are key to its success. Depending on the line of business, there may be none or only one link in the distribution of product or service to the customer, or there may be many links. To maintain control, the venture needs to have some influence with the distribution channel members.

The fewer the number of links a venture has in the distribution channel relative to competition and the industry norms and the more options it has for alternative channels of distribution, the greater is its potential for control. As the channels get longer, the venture loses control over to whom and how its products are presented, sold and serviced. If these aspects of the business are its distinctive competence or competitive advantage, loss of control can be fatal. As the channel members get larger in size and smaller in number, the venture must satisfy more of the channel members' wants in order to obtain their services.

The American Express traveler's check venture would never have grown so rapidly if it were not for the support it received through banks offering American Express traveler's checks to the public. Banks, many of which competed with American Express for banking business internationally, carry and promote traveler's checks to their customers. Because there were many banks that could provide distribution, and American Express offered traveler's checks with a reasonable fee for their service, American Express created a near monopoly in this business.

Citibank (formerly First National City Bank) was one of four other major issuers of traveler's checks in the 1970s and 1980s. Because Citibank was an aggressive bank competitor in most of its banking activities, other banks did not like to offer Citibank traveler's checks. Citibank had to settle for distribution through regional and community banks, and it had to provide a greater incentive to these banks to offer its traveler's checks.

Frank Perdue confronted a similar situation when he began to produce and sell chicken-dogs, hot dogs that were made from chicken. There already were several chicken-dog products on the market, and the refrigerator space in grocery stores was limited. Frank had to convince the buyers at retail stores to carry his chicken-based franks. He was sufficiently aware of the challenge that he personally called on buyers at grocery store retail chains and ran in-store promotions to support sales. His success with this product is directly linked to its acceptance by the retail-store buyers.

Suppliers. Somewhat less influential, but still a significant stakeholder group, are the suppliers of raw materials, equipment, technology, information, personnel, creativity, office supplies, etc. Every venture obtains inputs in the forms of goods and services from others. The larger the suppliers are relative to the venture's needs, the less the venture can influence suppliers to provide it with more of what it wants more quickly, with less error or waste, with more service or at a lower price. Yet, suppliers want ventures to stay in business and to grow so that they become larger and more profitable customers.

Some new venture managers nurture supplier relationships to obtain better service or more flexible payment terms. This is, in part, because some suppliers are willing to befriend the venture. Alternatively, it is possible to alienate a supplier. If all acceptable suppliers of a particular needed input choose not to provide the input, the venture has to create the input directly or alter its products and services so that it won't need the input. While this rarely happens, individual suppliers may increase price or reduce service levels to those customers they prefer not to serve.

Advertising agencies and public relations firms have been known to behave this way toward smaller clients that are particularly demanding. As the client hassles the agency over the service provided, the agency begins to eliminate the perks it provided to the client (e.g., a free business lunch). The agency may even begin to bill the client for agreed-upon services for which it might otherwise not have charged (e.g., a syndicated market research report that it already owned).

Whenever a venture is paying a professional, agent or agency for its expertise and time, it is possible for the service provider to provide less expertise and spend more time performing the service than is expected by the client. Professional and agency services frequently used by new ventures include the following:

- Accountants
- Advertising agencies
- Attorneys
- Auditors
- Copywriters
- Financial analysts
- Graphic artists
- Headhunters
- Investment bankers
- Market researchers
- Management consultants
- Media buyers
- Psychological testing firms
- Publicists
- Public relations specialists
- Venture consultants

Which professionals are used by your venture? How often? Are you monitoring the service provided? Are you satisfied with it? Why?

Since it is hard to determine the amount and quality of expertise provided and the time it took to provide the expertise without a direct comparison with other professional service providers, service that is overpriced, over-billed or of marginal quality may persist for weeks or months before it is dealt with directly—which often means hiring a new service provider and spending time and effort finding such a provider. Treating sources of supply as stakeholders in your venture can facilitate expense control and quality assurance.

Other Businesses. The fifth type of active external stakeholder in-volves other businesses that have ongoing relationships with the new venture. These businesses could be competitors or businesses with which the venture has an arrangement in the form of joint ventures, trading partnerships, licenses or importing and/or exporting rights.

How is it that competitors have a stake in a new venture? It would seem that their primary want from the venture is for it to go out of business. While this may be true in some instances, there are many situations in which competitors have a positive stake in what the venture does.

Do you ever shop for antiques? Or precious stones and jewelry? Do you like ethnic food? How about live-performance plays or comic clubs? In many cities these products and services are clustered together in a small neighborhood. Why? Do you think that these competitors that are in close proximity have a stake in the success of each other's business? I have asked many of them, and their answer is a uniform "yes." The reason they provide is that of "critical mass." Once an area becomes known for a type of product or service, it attracts many more customers who specifically want what it collectively has to offer. This contributes to the sales of all the competitors in the area.

If a business is in a new or growing industry, competition generally leads to greater industry growth. The pie of consumers gets bigger for all com-petitors to share. More people become aware of the new products, more referral business occurs, the products or services offered become more newsworthy and consumer interest and knowledge spread faster.

Some competitors may depend on a new venture's existence to provide incremental services or products that they do not want to provide. Smith & Hawken grew rapidly in spite of several significant competitive initiatives because it supplied a full line of garden supplies; competitors offered only the high-volume items. These competitors did have a stake in Smith &

Hawken's success. If Smith & Hawken had ignored this stakeholder relationship, they might have taken actions to attack the competition. Such an increase in competitive rivalry may well have reduced the profitability level for each of the firms competing without necessarily providing incremental benefit to customers.

Arrangements with other businesses that are not competitors generally exist for a collaborative reason. Collaboration occurs when both parties find it mutually beneficial to rely on the other party for some aspect of product manufacture or service delivery. This involves an agreed-upon arrangement, contract or letter of agreement between the businesses that specifies the nature of each firm's obligations and joint activities. Whether the arrangement is of a legal or informal nature, a dependency is created between the enterprises. Within this dependency, both players are stakeholders in the other's venture.

Several new ventures with which I have been involved have had licensing agreements with software companies or educational software providers. The letter of agreement always detailed what rights the licensee had to market, sell, deliver and/or use the licensed product. While licensees would often negotiate for universal rights, the licensers would limit the rights to what they felt could be reasonably serviced by the new venture until such time a license renewal was in order (typically three years).

If the licensers were too controlling, the licensees rarely gave the licensed product much attention. When licensers were too generous, they tended to become overly dependent on a licensee, leading to their desire to become more involved in the licensee's venture. Neither situation worked out to mutual advantage to the same degree as when ample rights were licensed, with modest control.

Identifying Active External Stakeholders

Obtaining the cooperation and buy-in of the many active external stakeholders is a complex and difficult challenge. Obtaining capital and adding production capacity, staff, operations and MIS seem easy in comparison to managing the many active external stakeholders associated with expansion. Without stakeholder buy-in and support, rapid growth is not possible. The active external stakeholder's stake in the new venture is as substantial as the active internal stakeholder's stake. While the jobs of the external stakeholders are not on the line in the same way as are the jobs of internal stakeholders, their money, energy and time are the cherished investments that they make in the new venture.

The following questions may assist you in identifying your venture's active external stakeholders. For each stakeholder identified, determine how important the stakeholder is to the venture's growth and profitability, what the stakeholder wants from the venture and what the venture offers the stakeholder.

Active External Stakeholder Analysis

	How are they important to us?	*What do they want from us?*	*What are they getting from us?*
• *Customers.* List the various types of customers—e.g., different types of individual buyers, buyers who are users versus nonusers, other businesses, wholesalers, schools, new businesses, repeat business, etc.			
• *Funding sources.* List all sources that apply—e.g., bankers, venture capitalists, investment firms, stock and bond holders, underwriters, personal lenders, family members and friends.			
• *Trade and distribution channel buyers* (e.g., distributors, wholesalers, retailers).			
• *Suppliers* (e.g., suppliers of raw materials, equipment, technology, information, personnel, creativity, office supplies).			

- *Other businesses* (e.g., competitors, joint ventures, trade partners, licensers, importers, exporters).

■———————————————————————————————————■

Now reflect on your venture's direction, particularly as it relates to its chosen destination and course. Given the venture's mission, vision and objectives, and with a solid understanding of its distinctive competence, which stakeholders are critical to its success over the next three to six months? Which stakeholders can block that success? List them.

_____   _____

_____   _____

_____   _____

_____   _____

Which stakeholders are critical to the venture's success over a one-year horizon? Over five years? List them.

One Year   *Five Years*

_____   _____

_____   _____

_____   _____

_____   _____

These are the key stakeholders to which you must devote at least half of the entire venture's energy in order to grow the business rapidly and profitably.

Active Internal Stakeholders

The active internal stakeholders include the new venture manager, other manager-owners and most employees. The venture partners, bosses and members of the board of directors (if there are any), direct subordinates, line employees, organized labor and contributed labor (e.g., voluntary help and family workers not paid a salary) are active internal stakeholders. These people, whether full-time exempt, full-time nonexempt or part-time employees gain a substantial portion of their livelihood from their activities in and contributions to the venture. The stake for some of these individuals will be modest; for others, the stake will be sufficiently great that if they were to leave the venture, its prospects for growing rapidly and profitably would be greatly diminished.

Partners. Partners come in many forms—co-owners, legal partners, general partners, limited partners and informal partners that are more like equal associates working in a corporation. Relationships with partners require ongoing maintenance—whether they be partners with equal shares in the venture's equity and success (and failure), partners with differing shares as a function of an agreed-upon distribution of equity, limited partners (those with no voting rights) or some form of nonequity partner (a partner in the venture's key decisions who is responsible for one or more key functions and is on salary or commission). Much like a marriage, partnerships are never as easy as one thinks. And just like divorce, they are always more difficult and painful to dissolve than either party imagines.

A partnership was once described to me as the relationship between a pilot and her plane. This analogy seemed strained at first; but upon reflection, it was on the mark. As a pilot, you need a checklist to review all sorts of things before each flight. Mistakes can be very costly, and routine maintenance is a necessity. When flying a plane, you try to use all of its potential (e.g., automatic pilot, radio communications and radar navigation) to your benefit. But if you misuse the equipment or push the craft beyond its limits, it can be unforgiving. Because it is forgiving most of the time, you are often led to a false sense of security. These attributes are claimed to be equally true of partnerships within a new venture.

To describe a partnership between two people as similar to that of a person and a machine may seem a bit odd. Yet, I have come to believe that *both parties in a partnership can benefit by viewing the relationship as one in which they are the machine and their partner is the human.* As the machine, what treatment do you want and need from the human? Once this is determined, you need to find ways of providing that *machine* treatment to your partner. Does this sound strange? Try it with your partners.

First check to see if both parties understand the venture's current issues, and then recheck this understanding before each major decision. The need for routine maintenance in the relationship is real. If you do not maintain the social and political sides of the relationship, it will begin to suffer. Know the limits of the relationship, and then don't exceed those limits. Most partnerships blow up when one partner violates the limits of the relationship once too often—whether it be by spending too much for a piece of equipment, taking money out of the venture for personal use or signing a contract with a supplier that the partners intended never to do business with again.

The unforgiving nature of mistakes rings true with most partnerships and partners. It is not that one person intends to be unforgiving—and people are rarely unforgiving the first or second time their limits are stretched. But too many tense times make for ongoing tense relationships. Tension makes it difficult to forgive.

If partnerships (as a legal form or within an incorporated venture) create critical stakeholders and relationships that are demanding to manage, why bother? The answers are many, not the least of which is the need for more capital to be provided by an equity partner and the need for specific expertise that the venture might not have. While partners often provide these resources as their contribution, their value as partners must go beyond money and knowledge. *Partnerships must also contribute to a shared sense of direction.*

Partnerships, in whatever legal form, must involve people as partners in a venture's mission, vision and objectives. Partners create and leverage a venture's distinctive competence. They share the values of the venture and create a corporate culture. For this to occur, partners must be people with whom you can talk, argue, debate and laugh.

Partners should make the good times better and the bad times easier to tolerate. This necessitates finding the right partner—not just any partner. Think of a partner as a significant internal stakeholder forever. Compare this to the external stakeholders, who may change, who may be substituted for other stakeholders and who can occasionally be ignored if they are not central to the key issues being addressed at a particular point in time.

Bosses.   As a new venture manager, you may have one boss, several bosses or even no bosses. You may also have an external board of directors to which you report. Without a boss, there is one less stakeholder to satisfy. A board of directors may be active or inactive, paid or voluntary. The legal responsibility of the board to provide oversight for the venture suggests that whatever its actual role, it is the higher authority to which the venture manager must answer.

For new ventures within existing organizations, there are always one or more bosses to whom the new venture manager reports. A boss might be actively involved in the new venture—requiring business plans, formal presentations and participation in decision making in return for corporate funding and political support within the organization. Or a boss may provide substantial autonomy. ("You run the venture, but keep me informed. I don't like surprises.")

You must determine with great clarity what it is the boss wants and work toward providing that want. If what is wanted cannot be provided, it needs to be discussed—today. As bosses become more removed from the activities of a new venture (which is often the case after a successful start-up), their wants may change or deviate from what is realistic for the venture. As key stakeholders in the venture, such bosses need as much relationship building and maintenance time as do partners.

After the Levi Strauss Company had launched its Tailored Classics menswear line of slacks, suit separates and suits, senior management moved their attention (and Levi financial resources) elsewhere. The Tailored Classics team was left to manage the fledgling venture. Within three years, the venture was sold; within six years, it was no longer a venture.

The Tailored Classics team failed to influence senior management or respond to their wants on several occasions. During its first year, their key competitor (Haggar) had increased sales over threefold in what was considered a slow-growth market. The market was there; unfortunately, Tailored Classics was not a big part of it. One reason for this was the lack of senior management support for the venture poststart-up. Obtaining senior management support is the new venture manager's ongoing responsibility, as is producing the product and selling it to consumers.

Direct Subordinates. The third category of active internal stakeholders is comprised of individuals who report directly to the new venture manager. New venture managers seek people with particular skills and aptitudes needed by the venture. Since most people hire others whom they believe will perform effectively, whom they think they will like and who espouse similar values and interests, the first few direct subordinates hired are apt to have wants that are fairly well understood by the new venture manager. As the number of direct reports increases, the potential for variations in values and interests increases. There is also an increased likelihood that the different direct reports will disagree with each other.

The differences in opinion that arise, coupled with differences in background and expertise, lead to conflicts over some venture issues. Conflicting views per se is not a significant problem for the new venture manager, as there are often technical expertise and informational reasons that explain different perspectives on an issue. What is important is for the new venture manager's direct reports to agree on the destination of the venture—its mission, vision and objectives. The efforts that new venture managers exert to clarify and build commitment among their direct reports will serve to align their wants with the venture's wants.

If disagreement occurs over the heading or course you have proposed, it is critical to discuss, debate and resolve this aspect of direction to everyone's satisfaction. The venture's distinctive competence needs to be believed and owned by all of the direct reports. If what is initially proposed is considered flawed, it is better to determine this early in the growth stage. Since there are many ways a venture can reach a destination, it is more important to obtain the direct reports' buy-in than it is to have them "go along with" your course and heading but not believe in it. They may unknowingly communicate their doubts to *their* direct reports. The more doubt that exists, the less people will be motivated and inspired to make the venture a success.

By determining a distinctive competence that is acceptable to people with different backgrounds and expertise, the top management echelon you create will more likely emerge into a team that can make whatever distinctive competence it believes in truly distinctive and truly a competence. Given management's influence on the venture, there is a greater likelihood that the values you espouse and the culture you hope to create will begin to permeate the venture's activities.

Line Employees.   Line employees are those employed by the venture who have direct responsibility for the aspects of the venture that generate revenues (with the exception of their bosses, who were mentioned earlier). *Line employees, as a group, are the venture.* While each person may be easily replaced, it will devastate a venture if many line employees leave or become alienated in a short period of time.

Line employees rarely have a common set of individual wants. Yet, as a group, they have wants that transcend their individual wants. What are these wants? If they can be diagnosed and understood, it may be possible to satisfy them as a routine aspect of conducting business.

Most line employees intuitively know that they are the core of the venture. They know that their stability is key to the venture's survival and that their collective efforts in pursuit of the organization's objectives are essential to venture growth and profitability. They also know that they are employees, not middle or senior management. While they may want to influence venture actions and decisions, they recognize that much of this authority lies with their bosses and the new venture manager.

This suggests that line employees want to feel valued, to have influence in the decisions that directly affect what they do on a daily basis and to have recognition and reward consistent with their being at the core of the venture. It also suggests that they do not want to control every aspect of the venture, nor do they believe that they should run the venture. Management often fears that labor wants to control all, so it yields little or no control. There is a middle ground. Find it.

Organized Labor. The fifth stakeholder group is organized labor—that is, the unions, trades and other groups of workers that function as a coalition and/or communicate their wants through a group representative. Organized labor's stake in an enterprise can be substantial, particularly if there are many other businesses nearby for which they might work. Their power is limited to the issues that are germane to their constituency (e.g., salary, benefits, working conditions, hours of work). By understanding and satisfying some of their wants and by involving them in select issues, it is possible to obtain their services without yielding control over key aspects of the venture.

Contributed Labor. In addition to paid employees, a venture may secure the services of volunteers—for example, interested retirees, family members and relatives. The services performed at no cost or at below-market rates is another form of contributed labor. Nearly every new venture manager interviewed indicated that some of the services and "employee" activities were contributed—not really paid for in the usual way. Some services were bartered; others were provided with the simple understanding that if things worked out, there might be some repayment in the future. Still other people contributed their efforts because they believed in the venture's mission and vision; being involved was their reward.

The following questions may assist you in identifying your venture's key active internal stakeholders. For all the stakeholders identified, determine how important they are to your venture's growth and profitability, what it is they want from the venture and what the venture is now giving them.

Active Internal Stakeholder Analysis			
	How are they important to us?	*What do they want from us?*	*What are they getting from us?*

- *Partners.* List the individuals you view as partners, either due to legal agreements or because the working arrangement makes you partners.

- *Bosses.* Include any formal bosses in the organizational hierarchy, members of the board of directors and others who have the power of a boss over the fate of the venture.

- *Direct subordinates.* List each one separately. Include line, staff, and administrative people.

- *Line employees.* Identify any subgroups that are likely to have different wants.

- *Organized labor.* List all unions, trade groups and coalitions that exist within the venture.

- *Contributed labor.* Identify those people who provide the venture with goods or services free, for barter or well below market rates.

Now reflect on the venture's direction, particularly as it relates to the chosen destination and culture you hope to create. Given its mission, vision and objectives—and your sense of values and corporate culture—which stakeholders are critical to its success over the next three to six months? List them.

_____   _____

_____   _____

_____   _____

_____   _____

Which stakeholders are critical to the venture's success over a one-year horizon? Over five years? List them.

One Year   *Five Years*

_____   _____

_____   _____

_____   _____

_____   _____

These are the stakeholders to whom you must devote about 40 percent of the entire venture's energy in order to obtain rapid growth and profitability. If you are not willing to do this, it is time to establish more modest growth goals.

Passive Internal Stakeholders

Passive internal stakeholders are employees who are affected by the actions of the new venture but who take a passive role in the leadership of the venture. This might include part-time workers, temporary employees and staff personnel in the less critical functional areas of the venture (e.g., public affairs or building services). These stakeholders might also be employees who are not strongly vested in the venture due to their lack of skills and unlikely career advancement.

As suggested earlier in Figure 6.1, passive internal stakeholders will only have a moderate stake in the venture. They are apt to have many of their primary wants satisfied outside of work. For these stakeholders, working in the new venture is a job, not a passion.

The importance of these people as stakeholders depends on their role in the venture. Banks often treat their tellers as if they are an unimportant component of the business. When customer service became a desirable competitive advantage, the role of the tellers became important, as it was the primary point of human contact with customers.

The same issue has arisen in the direct-mail business—customer service representatives (CSRs) are the primary point of human contact with the customer who places an order, has an inquiry or wishes to complain. While CSRs may not always be active internal stakeholders in the venture, their role with the customer makes them important stakeholders in the venture's growth. If such people directly affect the venture's customers, attending to their wants may be as critical as dealing with the venture partners.

Who are your venture's passive internal stakeholders? How important are they to the venture? What do they want from the venture, and what are they now getting from the venture?

Passive Internal Stakeholder Analysis

	How are they important to us?	*What do they want from us?*	*What are they getting from us?*
• *Staff workers.* List the areas separately.			
• *Part-time workers*			
• *Temporary help*			
• *Unskilled or semiskilled work force.* List the different jobs or positions separately.			

Passive External Stakeholders

The fourth category of stakeholders, those who are both passive and external, generally has a low stake in the venture. Some of these stakeholders do not care about the venture's failure or success. They will not interfere with the venture's leadership until they think that something the venture does (or does not do) affects their activities. At that time, these stakeholders will enact their own agendas and thrust them upon the venture for the betterment of their organization, society, social well-being or even the country itself. After the venture has attended to their issues, they return to their passive roles.

The five types of passive external stakeholders are (1) regulators, (2) local governments, (3) technology providers, (4) journalists and business analysts and (5) consumer interest groups. You can identify some of these stakeholders by considering the trends that are likely to affect your venture. (See chapter 1.)

Trends often attract the attention of regulators, governments, the press and consumer interest groups. Technology itself is often in transition, and it has been part of several business trends during the last 20 years. The passive external stakeholders will have distinct issues to which they want a venture to attend that derive from their respective missions.

Regulators. Regulators are people who work at one of the many regulatory agencies within the federal government, state and local governments and foreign countries. Some of the agencies that regulate various business activities include the Environmental Protection Agency, the Office of Health and Safety Administration, the Internal Revenue Service, the Food and Drug Administration, the Federal Aviation Administration and the Federal Communications Commission—to mention a few.

Each of these regulatory bodies has a charter to protect some things and/or people from abuses. *While it is possible to fight a regulatory body over a venture's rights, such activity is both costly and time-consuming.* A few new ventures have won such battles (e.g., Fred Smith at Federal Express). Most do not. You need an understanding of the regulations that affect your conduct of business as well as what it takes to conform to those regulations. If you decide to fight, choose your battles wisely. Fight only those issues that directly affect your venture's competitive advantage or distinctive competence. Let the other issues go.

Local Governments.   The community has a stake in your new venture. The venture and its employees use the streets and the sewers—and it pays taxes. This reflects the passive side of local government. The venture may also offer products or services to community members—is it doing this safely, quietly and without risk to the public? The venture employs people—is it paying a fair wage and protecting the human rights of its employees?

Local governments are likely to have many laws on their books that relate to what is appropriate and inappropriate in running a venture. Through the state, county or city agencies that exist to monitor businesses and protect the rights of the local citizens, these laws indicate that there are many different people in the community that have a minor stake in your enterprise. It is best to identify these stakeholders and give them what they want (if at all possible). The phrase "you can't fight city hall" seems to capture some practical advice for the new venture that is attempting to grow rapidly. Wait until the venture is much bigger before you fight, and then choose your battles carefully. Clint Eastwood fought local government in California successfully—after he won a local election and had starred in many films. He chose the time and place for the confrontation so that his chances of success were great.

Technology Providers.   A third type of passive external stakeholder is the technology provider. What technologies does your venture use? Production technologies? Information system technologies? Marketing technologies? Management technologies? Legal technologies?

The people providing these technologies have a stake in the venture. Some of the technologies used in the new ventures examined included computers (personal and mainframe), printers and photocopy equipment; software, such as specialized accounting programs, data processing programs and statistical analysis programs; educational technologies, such as cases, simulations and instructional aids; licensed manufacturing equipment and technologies; and licensed information bases. The list could go on for several pages. What technologies does your venture use?

Whenever a venture purchases or leases a technology, it is likely to need maintenance, upgrading and replacement over time. The technology provider is a key link for the servicing of the technology. As soon as the venture's technology lags behind that of the industry or competitors, it cannot rely on its technology to be an integral part of its competitive advantage or distinctive competence.

Travel agents who allow their systems to lag behind others in the field quickly experience a slow or no-growth situation. Old customers may remain, but new customers who have experienced faster or more convenient service elsewhere will not return. The same is true for bookstores with respect to on-line information about books in print and ordering information. If a bookstore is unable to locate and order a book for a new customer, it will probably not see that consumer very often.

Journalists and Business Analysts. Another passive external stakeholder group is the press. They seem to stay away when things are going well. When a tragedy occurs, they are omnipresent.

This need not be the case, however. Many reporters and analysts write favorable business press for newspapers and journals. Obtaining positive press requires that the venture view journalists and analysts as stakeholders in its mission. These stakeholders must be informed of the venture's reason for being, its vision and its destination. This may not lead to a story right away, but over time, nurturing the press can lead to more balanced reporting on the new venture's efforts.

Consumer Interest Groups. This fifth group of stakeholders covers the national and local organizations that have a stake in the community or culture they want to protect. If a venture's products are in some way connected to medicine or abortions, expect the Right to Life and Freedom of Choice groups to become active stakeholders. Or if the venture involves a building contractor, for example, in the Back Bay of Boston, expect the Back Bay Association and the Back Bay Architectural Society to be very interested in your work. Such consumer interest groups are often legally incorporated as nonprofit or not-for-profit corporations. They can and will take actions to support or impede your activities.

The number of consumer interest groups grew tenfold in the 1970s and tenfold again in the 1980s. In all likelihood, there are two or three such groups that will take an interest in your business activities if they know what you do and where you are headed. Since these interest groups are very focused and have volunteer members who are often self-righteous, knowing who the interest groups are and developing alliances with them can greatly reduce their disruptive effect on the venture and might even provide some advocacy of the venture's activities in the community. This may lead to more sales and profits, but it is more apt to lead to greater access to qualified labor and services within the community. It may also lead to fewer confrontations between the venture manager and local interest group officials.

Who are your venture's passive external stakeholders? How important are they to the venture? What do they want from the venture, and what are they getting from the venture?

■————————————————————————————————————■

Passive External Stakeholder Analysis

	How are they important to us?	What do they want from us?	What are they getting from us?
• *Regulators.* List the regulatory bodies that could or do regulate some of your venture's activities.			
• *Local governments.* Identify the local government agencies and laws that constrain your venture's practices.			
• *Technology providers.* List all of the nonproprietary technologies that the venture uses to conduct business (e.g., computing, software, manufacturing, accounting, marketing, payroll, information bases and so forth.)			
• *Journalists and business analysts.* List the media providers in your locale who are likely to report on venture activities, including newspapers, radio news, television news, magazines and industry analysts.			

- *Consumer interest groups.*
  List the areas in which your
  venture affects consumers
  and the community. Then
  identify any existing interest groups that focus on
  these areas.

Now reflect on your venture's direction, particularly as it relates to its chosen destination. Given its mission, vision and objectives, which of these passive stakeholders might become more active and affect the venture's chances of success over the next three to six months? Which stakeholders might become critical to the venture's success over a one-year horizon? Over five years? These are the key stakeholders to whom you must devote the remaining 10 percent of the venture's energy in order to reach the sweet spot. While it represents a small percentage of the venture's time, it is very likely a much larger percentage of your time as the new venture manager because passive stakeholders, when they become active, want to speak to the boss. Ignoring this want is very risky.

CHOOSING THE STAKEHOLDERS TO SATISFY

To the extent that you have been conducting the analyses suggested throughout chapter 6, you have already begun the process of determining which stakeholders you want to satisfy and how you can satisfy them. Since there are many stakeholders whose wants are not always compatible, we need a way of selecting which stakeholders will be given priority. To do this, use the SPOT analysis developed in chapter 3.

The SPOT analysis involved first identifying the venture's strengths, problems, opportunities and threats and then using this information to answer the question, "What can we do now?" With the list of possible actions that are viable answers to this question in hand, determine which actions are most likely to lead the venture toward its mission, vision and objectives.

For each of these actions, who are the key stakeholders? What is it they want, and what is it the venture is giving them now? It is these stakehold-ers—those who are along the course from where the venture is now to where it wants to go—who must be satisfied. They must be allowed to feel their positive stake in the new venture—and the loss of that stake if progress is not made along the course from where the venture is now to where you are leading it.

With the knowledge of whom to satisfy, the question becomes, "How does the venture satisfy key stakeholders so that it prospers?" We begin to explore some possible answers to this question in chapter 7.

7

Influencing and
Embracing Key
Stakeholders

In chapter 6 we suggested a framework for identifying the many possible stakeholders in a new venture. For a new venture to influence its key stakeholders, embracing those who are most important to rapid growth, new venture managers need to identify the specific wants that each key stakeholder has that the venture might satisfy.

The process of influencing key stakeholders is a dynamic one, as the key stakeholders and their wants often change during periods of rapid growth. Effectively influencing stakeholders involves attending to and acting on issues related to the following three interrelated areas that have been developed in previous chapters:

1. Questions of *direction* (discussed in chapter 5)

2. Questions of *buy-in* (discussed in chapter 6)

3. Questions of *capability* (discussed in chapters 1 through 4)

TWO KEYS TO SUCCESS

After dozens of interviews with struggling new venture managers, two areas emerged as the biggest challenges. New venture managers consistently indicated that there were two omnipresent areas needing their attention.

1. *Identifying* the points of contact between the venture's activities and the stakeholders' activities and then effectively *influencing* the behavior of the stakeholders through the venture's actions and inactions

2. *Finding* or *creating* areas in which the interests of the venture and the interests of stakeholders are consistent with the direction and capabilities of the venture.

Each of these areas is discussed in this chapter by means of a case situation, followed by suggestions for attending to the area of management concern.

IDENTIFYING AND INFLUENCING STAKEHOLDERS

Points of Contact

Chapter 6 provided a framework for identifying the stakeholders in a venture's activities. Using this framework, a relatively small number of stakeholders are likely to be critical to any particular issue being confronted at a point in time. These are the key stakeholders. For each of these key stakeholders, identify *every point of contact, when* the contact takes place, *where* the contact takes place and *how* the contact takes place.

Points of contact go beyond the advertising message and media. Is there a sales call, a point-of-sale display or completion of a warranty card? What about contacts with the customer after the sale, such as dealing with the personnel in the customer service unit, receiving monthly statements or bills and purchasing replacement parts or supplies?

To detect many of the points of contact, *become a consumer of your product.* Trace the process in detail—from initial exposure to the product through purchase, use, the discarding of product remains to repurchase of the product or a substitute product. Consumers think and feel many things about a product before purchase, and they then rethink these things in light of their experience with the product.

List five points of contact between your business and a customer.

1.

2.

3.

4.

5.

Have you included points of contact that occur through advertising, publicity, personal selling, direct marketing and other communication mechanisms?

6.

7.

8.

9.

Have you included points of contact that occur postpurchase, such as completing a warranty card; referring the product to an associate, friend or neighbor; or reading the instruction booklet?

10.

11.

12.

What if something goes wrong? Have these points of contact been identified?

13.

14.

Each of these points of contact provides you with an opportunity to influence the customer.

The Consumer Purchase Process

Figure 7.1 identifies the process that a person goes through before making a thoughtful purchase. While not all steps are discrete for every purchase, consumers progress up the ladder before making a purchase or repurchase. They also stop climbing—or fall off of the ladder—when the messages they receive do not reinforce their initial direction.

Consumer points of contact start with awareness—the occasion when a consumer first understands that a particular product exists. If a consumer's awareness of a product is linked to some conscious (or unconscious) want, he or she becomes interested. In the absence of a want, a consumer may remain aware of an offering but will not be interested in the product. He or she will have little ability to recall information about the product unless specifically asked.

Figure 7.1 Steps in Purchase Decisions

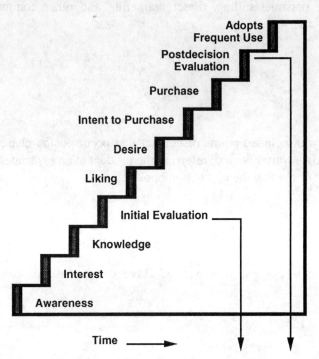

Once awareness is linked to a want (a goal of good advertising), consumers become interested in the product. This interest may be active, leading to specific efforts to obtain more information and gain knowledge about the product. Or the interest may be passive, whereby additional knowledge of the product seeps into a consumer's mind due to its unsolicited availability. Automobile ads focus on stimulating consumer awareness and interest—knowledge acquisition is generally a small part of the ad. A consumer must visit a new-car showroom or seek out someone who already is knowledgeable about a particular car to obtain detailed information.

In contrast, toothpaste ads try to make the public aware, interested and informed of the product's unique attributes in the short space of a 30-second ad. This does not mean that consumers actually take three steps forward in their purchase process just because an ad provides them with that opportunity. Most ads need to be seen several times before consumers can accurately recall the knowledge elements in the ads. An ad may require three or four points of contact before it accomplishes its goal—even for the consumer who wants the product.

Once consumers have some knowledge about a product, they evaluate the product. This evaluation may not be accurate or fair from the manufacturer's point of view, but it is the consumers' judgment nonetheless. As Figure 7.1 suggests, this evaluation might be negative, leading to disinterest, or it might be positive, leading to "liking" the product.

Initial evaluation may take place without any additional points of contact (as may occur with a toothpaste purchase), or it may involve a trial or sample of the product (as with an automobile). Cosmetic and perfume manufacturers often let consumers try their products before purchase. Apple Computer allowed its target consumers to "test drive a Macintosh" by permitting them to take a computer home overnight. Soap manufacturers provide samples of their new products (Lever 2000 soap bars were given to millions of people in 1991) to overcome consumers' loyalty to other soap products.

Even after a positive evaluation, there may be several additional points of contact before purchase. People do not necessarily move from liking a product to purchasing it without additional stimulation. To progress from liking something to desiring it is equivalent to going from a thoughtful analysis to an emotional yearning.

People often like the latest fashions in clothes, but they may not desire the clothes until they see them on someone they admire. You may like Perrier, but you may not desire it until you can sip it at the bar of your favorite restaurant. And if the bartender does not mention Perrier specifically, you might just order club soda or mineral water instead.

What are the points of contact for your product that move consumers from liking the product to desiring it? What then moves them to conviction—and intent to buy? Many of our intentions do not lead to the actual behavior intended. Why? It may be that we do not have the opportunity, the resources or the time. Or maybe we just got sidetracked and forgot until the opportunity had passed. When a purchase does occur, what moved the consumer from intent to purchase to actual purchase? What is the point-of-sale contact?

Many people stop their analysis of consumer behavior at the purchase event. This is a gross mistake. Product evaluation occurs—along with a mental process called postdecision dissonance—at and immediately following the point of sale. People often regret their decisions as soon as they have made them. They have expended their resources in one way, precluding expending them in other ways.

This leads to an initial feeling of loss. To overcome this feeling, people begin to look for the good in the decision that they made. They want to prove to themselves that they made a wise choice. Are you giving people a little something extra to feel good about at or just following the point of sale? During this early postpurchase period, people pay more attention to a product's ads, service agreement, warranty form and other points of contact with the product or its delivery system than they did before their purchase.

A positive postpurchase evaluation is essential for rapid growth. Customers are eager to talk about recent purchases. They often encourage others to try the product at this time because they are looking for reinforcement of their decision. New venture managers need to ensure that the postpurchase evaluation involves additional positive points of contact. A handshake at the end of a purchase or offering a business card or piece of candy can make the postpurchase evaluation more favorable. A follow-up call from the salesperson asking if everything is satisfactory or a cents-off coupon toward the next purchase are other ways additional points of contact can influence the purchase evaluation. *What additional points of contact is your venture creating to influence the postpurchase evaluation?*

Purchase and evaluation lead consumers to another decision point. Consider the following choices that consumers make and how you might influence them to take actions that lead to more business:

- Do they use the product?
- Do they talk to others about the product?
- Do they recommend the product?
- Do they become active users and/or repeat purchasers?
- Do they encourage others to use the product?
- Do they speak highly of the product?
- Are they seen using the product (becoming a point of product exposure)?

Identifying the points of contact between the new venture and its customers is detailed work. It involves understanding what the firm is doing with its other products and how they might relate to the new venture's product and target customers. It involves understanding how advertising and media exposure affect target customers. It also involves understanding how the channels of distribution and promotional activities are affecting the consumers' decision-making processes.

Reflect on the many points of contact between your venture's product and its target consumers. Consider these questions in your analysis of the purchase process of consumers:

- How might people first become aware that the product exists? Advertising? Word of mouth? Promotional displays? Observing its use by someone else?

- What is this experience like?

- Is the product observed or presented in a favorable light? The most favorable light?

- How often is an exposure experience repeated or observable each week?

- Do consumers link the new product with other products or services the business offers?

- Is the new product's image likely to be affected by the firm's other activities?

- If so, are the people responsible for those activities stakeholders in your venture's success?

- What additional points of contact occur that can potentially influence the consumer to purchase or use the product?

- What points of contact might move a consumer from awareness of the product to interest in it? From interest to knowledge acquisition? To a positive initial evaluation? To liking the product? To desiring it? To an intention to purchase it? To a positive postpurchase evaluation? To adoption and frequent use?

- What additional points of contact are associated with servicing the product?

- What points of contact lead to repeat purchases?

Influencing Behaviors at the Points of Contact

Having identified the points of contact, it is worthwhile to explore the objective of each contact. *Why* does the contact take place? Does the contact lead to *positive and effective outcomes?*

The ultimate purpose of any contact with any stakeholder is to influence the behavior of the person being contacted. As implied in Figure 7.1, even a simple contact, such as an advertisement intended to generate awareness or interest, is a stepping-stone to the ultimate goal: influencing someone to do something.

What behaviors are we trying to influence? Ventures want consumers to purchase, use and repurchase their products. In addition, ventures want consumers to refer people to them and encourage others to try their products. Ventures might also want consumers to use the products publicly and in their intended manner. This list of desired behaviors is becoming quite long, but do ventures use their points of contact to influence all of these behaviors in the desired direction and in a timely manner?

New venture managers also want to influence the behaviors of other stakeholders. Which ones and in what ways? To answer these questions, start by looking for the points of contact with each key stakeholder and then examine the behaviors you are trying to influence. The section in chapter 2 that addresses a venture's profit-loss dynamics ("How do we make money in this business?") and the venture's behavioral goals are particularly helpful here. Reflect on your understanding of how the business works and your goals in order to identify whose behaviors you want to influence and in what ways.

Consumer Package Goods.   Consider the plight of the manufacturers of consumer package goods. Not only must they influence consumers to try and use their products, but they must obtain distribution first. How do they get their new products carried by retail stores? Each store has a limited amount of shelf space and a fixed number of shelf facings—all of which are fully occupied.

First, the retailers must be influenced to carry the product. And why should they? A strong, convincing answer must be provided to this question—or there will be no sale.

To obtain rapid sales through retail outlets, a new product must be in a prime location, it should be well stocked and it must have easily noticed shelf facings. This means that some other product will get less shelf space or fewer shelf facings once your product is carried. There probably is an advertising account executive and a brand manager responsible for the other product that is going to lose space and a facing—both of whom already have an ongoing relationship with the retail store.

Influencing a retail store to support your product over the competition's product is a difficult challenge. Once this challenge is met, and if initial success is achieved, the product will have to be restocked more often, thereby requiring more attention and action on the part of the retailer's staff.

How do you increase the likelihood that these events will occur? It helps to know what you are trying to accomplish and the nature of the resistance. *The process of influencing and embracing those you intend to influence begins with developing an understanding of a stakeholder's position—from the stakeholder's point of view.*

L'eggs. L'eggs was able to obtain distribution channel support with outstanding success. Stockings and panty hose had traditionally been sold through department stores and specialty stores, not grocery stores or pharmacies. L'eggs decided to pursue this different distribution channel.

To overcome the "fixed-space" constraint, L'eggs provided additional shelf space through a novel display that was cylindrical and that could be rotated by consumers. This display could be placed at the end of an aisle or in any location of about three square feet. The number of shelf facings was greater than comparable linear shelving by more than 50 percent, even before the cylinder was rotated. By involving the consumer in altering the shelf facings by rotating the cylinder, the number of facings actually increased threefold. Not only did L'eggs gain access to a new distribution channel for its category of product, it did so without reducing the retailer's traditional shelf space.

L'eggs' novel packaging, intensive advertising and creative channel support resulted in one of the century's rapid-growth success stories. More than ten years later, Frookies accomplished the same thing with a new product—a fruit-juice-based cookie. Frookies obtained shelf facings in grocery stores by providing a freestanding shelf display—for placement near the checkout counter.

All rapid-growth success stories do not require new ideas—some involve an existing idea applied in another way. But before any idea can be applied to a problem, you must be clear on the problem you are trying to solve—

which often means identifying whose behavior you want to influence and what their situation is from their point of view.

As you reflect on the key issues facing your venture today, identify the key stakeholders in the outcomes of each issue. What behaviors do you want to see in these stakeholders to support your venture's growth objectives? Consider the following questions for each significant stakeholder:

- What is their stake in the issue?

- What do they need from the venture?

- What do you need from them—in terms of end results?

- What might precede the end result that would also be desired? What might precede that?

- Define all the behaviors needed to get from the current situation to the venture's objective.

- What things might block the stakeholder from behaving in the desired way?

- How might these barriers be viewed by the stakeholder?

- How might these barriers be reduced?

- Who needs to do what for a barrier to be eliminated?

- How might the venture influence the parties that can reduce barriers?

AREAS THAT LINK THE VENTURE'S DIRECTION AND CAPABILITIES WITH STAKEHOLDERS' WANTS

New venture managers should consider the following questions each day:

- What does the venture want?

- What do the stakeholders want?
- What can the venture do?

By asking and exploring possible answers to these questions, new venture managers can enact a diagnostic and discovery process that helps them facilitate the changes necessary for the venture to obtain rapid and profitable growth. In Figure 7.2, each of these questions is associated with a circle. Each circle signifies all of the thoughts and behaviors that are answers to one of the questions—as the answers relate to the specific issue being analyzed.

The model in Figure 7.2 has its greatest impact on your thinking when it is used as a tool for diagnosis and discovery. Figuratively, you record the answers to each question in that question's circle. From these initial answers come new insights as to how you can proceed more effectively.

The answers you provide are often idiosyncratic to the situation, but the process of asking these questions and reflecting on the answers is valid and useful to many people and situations. The answers tend to guide your subsequent behaviors much the way a physician's diagnostic questions guide the physician's behaviors. The patient's responses to the physician's questions and actions provide information that may lead to additional questions and discovery.

The model shown in Figure 7.2 is called the W-cubed (W^3) model to signify the three "what" questions that new venture managers ask themselves repeatedly in their leadership efforts. Using graphic notation, W^3 is shown as three overlapping circles. The overlap between the circles indicates that the most effective ideas will simultaneously address the three diagnostic questions:

1. What does the venture want?

2. What do the stakeholders want?

3. What can the venture do?

Business issues are most likely to receive attention and be effectively resolved when the issues fit the multiple goals of different constituencies within the evolving environments—and when the managers are capable of addressing them.

The W x W x W symbolism communicates the importance of simultaneously answering the three diagnostic questions. As with any equation involving only multiplication, if any of the elements is zero, the product is zero. *Finding answers to each of the three questions that are consistent and*

Figure 7.2   The W-cubed Model

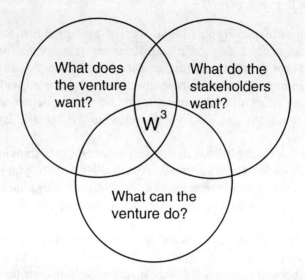

compatible with the answers to the other two questions is critical to the growth and profitability of your new venture.

What Does the Venture Want?   Venture and personal goals define the set of valued outcomes that you intend to seek. The question of whose goals will be accomplished by attending to various issues is a critical one.

Within the context of the W^3 model, you need to ask the question, *Who is 'the new venture'?* It is common and necessary for new venture managers to have more than one point of reference when thinking about issues. Such reference points might include thinking about the situation as a founder of the new venture, as the manager of the business, as a peer of the other venture partners or as an individual.

New venture managers are responsible for a venture's activities that go beyond any single individual's wants. What people want for themselves in their career may be different from what they want in the position they occupy. By asking the question, *What is meant by 'the new venture'?*, managers can focus their diagnosis on a single entity at a time.

"The new venture" could mean "you" personally. "The new venture" could also be the new venture manager in his or her role within the venture. "The new venture" could mean the entire business or even the entire organization. As you may suspect from the existence of more than one perspective on what is "the new venture," the W^3 model is best applied to one perspective at a time. It can then be reapplied to other perspectives on an issue if desired.

The process of identifying what the venture wants may also take the form of eliminating what it does not want—by eliminating some alternatives that are not consistent with the venture's direction. In some situations, it is easier to identify the things that the venture does *not* want—which might be accomplished by reflecting on past actions to identify the not-so-successful situations and events. Determining what is wanted in the future requires knowing or envisioning possibilities, many of which are not part of a venture's experiences.

Asking such questions as *Who is the new venture?* and *What doesn't the new venture want?* are examples of how W^3 is used to discover things you might already know but not realize. Each of the three diagnostic questions in the model can be thought of as a *leading question*—one that is easily remembered and used to suggest other questions (*following questions*) germane to the leading question. When leading questions cannot be easily answered, following questions tend to emerge. By considering the following questions, you can frequently generate interesting alternative answers to the leading questions.

What Do the Stakeholders Want?   The second set of ideas involves the various stakeholders in the venture—those individuals, groups and organizations that have a stake in the actions the venture takes. The number and divergent interests of the various stakeholders make their assessment problematic. Yet, by asking the questions, *What do the stakeholders want?* and *Who are the key stakeholders for this particular issue?,* you can simplify your environmental analysis without losing much rigor.

Stakeholder research has examined these questions and supports the importance of articulating the multiple "theys" and their wants. It is the stakeholders who create the environments that new venture managers subsequently perceive. By determining who the relevant "theys" are and what they want, you are identifying the possible barriers or constraints with which you will have to contend.

Stakeholder information can be collected by asking the various parties questions about their wants, not just once but periodically throughout each year. Obtaining such information does not seem to obligate the venture to satisfy the wants of these stakeholders; instead, it identifies areas where there could be mutual benefits and areas that might be best avoided.

As suggested by the overlapping circles shown in Figure 7.2, the easiest ideas to implement are those that can satisfy the venture's wants and the wants of the key stakeholders. The greater the overlap (i.e., the greater the consistency of the goals of affected parties), the greater is the ease of implementing ideas. To the extent that some of the venture's goals are not consistent with the goals or constraints imposed by relevant others (i.e., the two circles are not concentric), your efforts to attain these inconsistent goals are likely to be stalled, compromised or made ineffective by people in the environments that have a stake in the issues being addressed.

What Can the New Venture Do? Developing an understanding of the business unit's strengths and capabilities is central to the growth of a new venture. It is similarly essential to strategic thinking. Organizations and individuals perform more effectively when they are predominantly using established capabilities. This does not imply that new strengths should not be developed; rather, the development of new capabilities should consume a relatively small amount of energy so as not to distract the venture and its employees from leveraging existing strengths. The costs of developing new strengths is high relative to the cost of using a developed strength to achieve growth and profitability objectives.

As introduced in chapter 2, a widely used tool for accomplishing an analysis of what the venture can do is SPOT. SPOT involves examining the venture's strengths (S), problems (P), opportunities (O) and threats (T). The SPOT model encourages new venture managers to assess their venture's capabilities as part of a detailed analysis of their business situation. It does not replace other assessment tools such as MIS reports, accounting information and market research. Rather, the insights gained through such assessments can be recorded on a SPOT chart as a way of visually presenting the analysis.

SPOT should be used in the same diagnostic and discovery manner as W^3. Its four elements—collectively—can provide meaningful insights into which business actions are likely to be more viable. Through conducting a SPOT analysis, you develop an understanding of your venture's capabilities for pursuing various opportunities, overcoming problems and avoiding or minimizing threats. When you apply a capabilities analysis to a specific business situation, you are assessing the feasibility that you and the venture can handle a particular possibility effectively.

Target Markets and Competitive Advantage

If the three W^3 circles were frequently concentric, there would be little need to target or focus a venture's energies on accomplishing some goals while denying action on others. All of the venture's wants would be compatible with its stakeholders' wants and the venture's capabilities. Over time, everything could be accomplished. As this is rarely the situation, it is important to identify the area of probable overlap. This area is often described as a *target market*—the market of stakeholders, including customers, that most likely wants what the venture wants and can offer.

As suggested earlier by the phrase "the essence of strategy is denial," growing a business rapidly requires that many things be denied. The issues that do make your agenda are only a small number of those that could have made the agenda. New venture managers who can keep issues moving— often by understanding when their initial solutions are not apt to satisfy all three W^3 questions—are more likely to find solutions that do satisfy all three questions.

While the W^3 model stimulates thinking around many different wants, stakeholders and capabilities, there will always be a limited set of ideas that simultaneously satisfy the three questions. Many of these ideas will not be immediately apparent. This is graphically suggested in Figure 7.3 by the three circles having no area in common. Creativity is often required, particularly in the ways in which new venture managers define and interpret issues, to shift the analysis of the situation in ways that lead to some useful "overlaps."

Obtaining overlap can be accomplished by expanding the venture's wants (by making the circle with "What does the venture want?" bigger). It can also be done by expanding the venture's capacity or capabilities (by making the circle with "What can the venture do?" bigger). Or it might involve identifying some additional customer wants that were not previously considered (by making the circle with "What do the stakeholders want?" bigger). It might also involve some combination of these three ideas.

Finally, you may have to redefine the situation so that the various stakeholders view it differently, thereby finding some areas of overlap or agreement. This involves moving the circles closer together. It is this last alternative that holds the most promise for growing a business rapidly and profitably.

Figure 7.3 The W-cubed Model with No Stakeholder Overlap

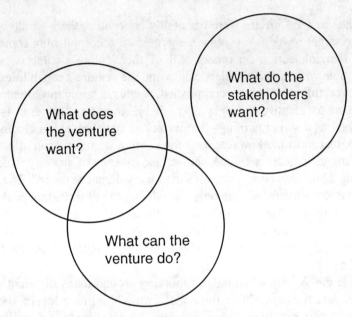

Focusing on a target that satisfies the three questions is not enough to ensure success. *Being able to satisfy the wants of relevant others does not necessarily mean that the venture will be given the opportunity to do so.* People may get their wants satisfied elsewhere.

The concept of competitive advantage is relevant here because the venture is in a mutual-choice situation. If consumers and other significant "theys" select you and you select them, then a competitive advantage is necessary. Just as the venture needs a competitive advantage as a business, every issue that involves getting at the center W^3 for resolution will benefit by there being a clear reason why the stakeholders involved in that issue want to do business with you.

APPLYING W^3 TO EMBRACE KEY STAKEHOLDERS

Through observation of new venture managers, we have developed a number of insights into applying W^3 that reinforce the belief that W^3 is a personal discovery mechanism that can improve a new venture manager's capacity to dramatically grow a business profitably. New venture managers find it easy to use W^3 as a diagnostic tool—they ask the three questions and generate answers based on a moderate amount of exploration and reflection. They often summarize the various ideas that emerge through their analyses in the form of W^3 and SPOT charts. If there is substantial convergence among the W^3 questions, they make fairly clear choices among their business opportunities and take decisive actions.

As you might guess, a high degree of convergence among the W^3 questions is not particularly common for new venture managers dealing with issues of rapid growth. *What does occur is the identification of the many wants that the venture has, the many different stakeholders in the venture's activities, the stakeholders with different and often incompatible wants and the limited set of new venture can-do's.* Now what?

Rollerblades

One example of "now what" is the activity of Rollerblade, the first company to manufacture skates with wheels in a line and to market them to American consumers. In 1987 Rollerblade had annual sales of about $3 million and 16 full-time employees. While skates with in-line wheels could be used by anyone interested in skating, they were predominantly used by hockey skaters. To grow rapidly, Rollerblade knew that it would have to either create a new outdoor sport that would be attractive to hundreds of thousands of people or replace the existing rollerskates that had parallel wheels with the Rollerblade model. But why not try to do both?

Attacking both markets (creating both a new sport and a product to substitute for traditional roller skates) involved too many different consumer stakeholders with substantially different wants to be satisfied with one product. Rollerblades lacked the stability of traditional roller skates. (They are even a bit dangerous until the skater has developed moderate skill in skating.)

Much of the traditional roller-skate market is comprised of children and teenagers. These consumers buy low- to moderate-priced skates and are conscious of the risks of roller skating. The purchaser of traditional roller skates is often not the end user. The more professional market for traditional roller skates is difficult to penetrate due to its existing affiliations with the manufacturers of skates.

In contrast, the market for a new sport could include whomever Rollerblade decided to target, with whatever message they wanted to convey. What would make the Rollerblade skates attractive, and what types of consumers did Rollerblade want to find them attractive?

The identification and diagnosis of possible consumers for rollerblades went through several iterations. Many questions were posed: Should Rollerblade focus on athletes (e.g., hockey players or professional skaters)? Should the company position rollerblading as a competitive, playful and/or fitness activity? Depending on the positioning, which competitors and noncompetitive companies might have a stake in Rollerblade's success? Are there companies that might want to associate with rollerblading as a new and upcoming fitness and sport activity? Who are they, and how can Rollerblade obtain their interest? What is it that such companies want from Rollerblade? Can Rollerblade give it to them, and is it consistent with Rollerblade's chosen direction?

These were the questions that occupied the managers at Rollerblade. Their marketing budget was modest (about $200,000) for a national consumer campaign. It was not possible to pull thousands of consumers into retail stores to buy Rollerblades through traditional advertising on this level of budget. By asking and reasking the question "What can we do?", Rollerblade generated a variety of alternatives to reach different possible target consumers. They also explored possibilities of collaboration with other organizations to obtain exposure—to get Rollerblades noticed. They realized that if they actively sought more stakeholders in their success, they could reach more consumers at a lower price than if they were to try to do it alone.

What did Rollerblade do to reach $100,000,000 in retail sales in four years? First, they made some directional decisions: they tried to create a new sport that would focus on the 15- to 35-year-old consumer market; they emphasized how much fun it is to rollerblade; and they tied the product to an action, fitness image rather than to a competitive image.

Then Rollerblade sought relationships with others to promote Rollerblades in a manner consistent with their mission and vision. They wanted to attract media attention. To accomplish this, they gave Rollerblades to celebrities and professional athletes—people with high profiles that were likely to pass the word along (e.g., well-known cyclists, skiers, walkers, runners, surfers, pizza-delivery services, ice skaters).

Next, they sought cross-promotional tie-ins with companies that shared their audience (e.g., General Mills, Pepsi and Procter & Gamble). Their first tie-in was a promotion with Golden Grahams cereal. Rollerblade provided 1,000 pairs of skates in return for the display of their product on six million cereal boxes as a promotional giveaway. By linking excitement with fitness, Rollerblade attracted the kind of attention they wanted.

The Need for Analysis

The Rollerblade example suggests that the W^3 and SPOT tools are likely to be used in an ongoing manner. Rollerblade did not know who all of its stakeholders were, nor their wants, until it began to clarify what it wanted and what it could do. As this occurred, the new venture managers began to set more priorities and clarify their wants, stakeholder wants and their ability to deliver.

Consider the following questions as you examine the directions, stakeholders and capabilities of your new venture:

- Which of the venture's goals are most important to you? To the other partners? To the customers?

- Which goals are less important?

- Which stakeholders are most important to you?

- Which stakeholders are most likely to affect goal accomplishment?

- Are the wants the stakeholders have really important wants for the venture to be satisfying?

- Are the strengths the venture has really germane to what the venture now wants?

- Are the areas the venture wants to develop important now or at some future time?

The questioning continues with incremental answers to many of the questions. When information is lacking, an agenda is often created for further exploration, including discussions with of some of the stakeholders.

Even after exploration, some people are unable to identify opportunities or a clear choice. What we observe at this stage is a redefinition of the venture's goals and its relationship with some of the stakeholders. The new venture managers are also redefining their roles within the venture. This redefinition requires a fair amount of energy and openness to alternative ways of thinking about situations.

In the more productive instances, people use this impasse as an opportunity to reflect broadly on the venture—leading to some exciting new developments. Some people get stuck in neutral. They limit their exploration, they accept their current situation as permanent and they disengage. They have stopped trying to find the overlap among the three questions in W^3 and have settled for less stellar performance. This stuck-in-neutral stage can pass—but not without adding incremental energy to the system.

When exploration and redefinition of the situation do not lead to viable options, the bargaining process begins. ("That may be what the venture wants, but what can it get?" or "This may be what that stakeholder wants, but what will he or she accept?") New venture managers begin to focus their energies on some of the venture's wants, on select stakeholders and on the venture's most important "can do now's." The goal is to resolve issues faced by the venture in ways that lead to profitable growth.

To start this analysis, we must examine the wants of the different stakeholder groups:

- How much and what kind of direction is wanted by active versus passive stakeholders and by external versus internal stakeholders?

- Which stakeholders are most interested in the venture's destination, heading and course as well as its management style?

New venture managers need to provide their various stakeholders with enough of what they want *and* keep those directional fires alive in themselves and the venture for the sweet spot to be reached.

Directions Wanted by Different Stakeholders

Leading a new venture would be burdensome and unpleasantly difficult if all stakeholders were equally interested in the various directions provided by new venture managers. Communicating destination, course and management style to many different stakeholders in ways they both understand and support is more than a venture in its early growth stage can possibly handle.

Fortunately, some stakeholders are interested in some aspects of the venture's direction and are not interested in others. By focusing on the different aspects of direction wanted by each stakeholder group, it is possible to provide each group with information appropriate to its needs. You can also seek the necessary involvement of select stakeholders in changes in direction, while maintaining control of the venture's activities.

Active External Stakeholders.   The active external stakeholders are the venture's customers, funding sources, trade and distribution channel buyers, suppliers and other businesses that have relationships with the venture. *The more salient wants of the active external stakeholders are with respect to the venture's course.* These stakeholders are interested in how and whether the new venture will provide them with products and service, a satisfactory return on their equity or with orders for the materials and services they provide the venture so that the venture can produce its products and services. A new venture's course is best described by its distinctive competencies (and to a lesser extent, by its competitive advantage). The venture can persist in reaching its destination through continually leveraging its distinctive competence. The primary importance of course to the active external stakeholders is shown graphically in Figure 7.4 by the word "course."

The second area of direction of some interest to active external stakeholders is the venture's destination. The venture's mission and vision can provide these stakeholders with some comfort about what the venture might become in the future. If active external stakeholders accept the venture's destination, they are more likely to remain stakeholders during difficult as well as easy times.

The stakeholders who are satisfied by the venture's course, but not its destination, are likely to be stakeholders only when there are no problems to resolve. For example, customers are more apt to tolerate a service problem, or the need to return a faulty product, when they view the venture as providing a useful and wanted product and believe that the venture's destination is a worthy one.

Tylenol survived its product-tampering threat because it obtained the support of the consumer for its efforts to solve the problem as well as for its overall mission—which was to provide a pain reliever that was an alternative to aspirin. People believed that Tylenol management was doing

Figure 7.4 Directions Wanted by Stakeholders

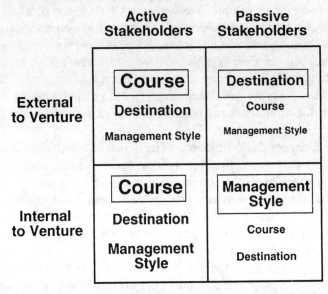

everything they could to provide a safe product and prevent such abuse in the future in its pursuit of its mission.

Direction as defined by management style is generally of little importance to most of the venture's active external stakeholders. Customers, funding sources, buyers, suppliers and other business affiliates will probably continue doing business with the new venture independent of its internal culture. Yet, some of the trends suggested in chapter 1 could imply that there may be some active external stakeholders who will voice their opinions about the internal operations of some new ventures. For example, the growing desire by consumers to "save our society" implies pressures for new ventures to behave in an environmentally and socially responsible manner. An internal culture that is wasteful or ecologically insensitive might be boycotted by a portion of its target consumers who believe that all firms should be assisting in the effort to save our society. Alternatively, by being ecologically conservative, a venture may attract the business of those individuals that value this approach.

Active Internal Stakeholders. The active internal stakeholders include the venture partners, bosses, the new venture manager's direct subordinates, line employees, organized labor and contributed labor. Each of these stakeholders will be interested in all aspects of the venture's direction: its course, destination and management style.

Of greatest interest is the venture's course—its distinctive competence. If the active internal stakeholders do not know and accept the venture's distinctive competence, they will not be able to communicate it effectively to the active external stakeholders (e.g., customers and buyers). In determining the venture's distinctive competence, as in suggesting a course for a trip, it is critical to get the buy-in of those who are going along, particularly if you need their help to reach the destination.

Of nearly equal importance to the active internal stakeholders is the venture's destination and management style. Both of these aspects of the venture affect the active internal stakeholders on a daily basis. Knowing the venture's destination, particularly as it relates to the venture's vision, provides the inspiration to continue. Goals and objectives define the areas of greatest importance, thereby directing people's attention to those areas that are apt to lead to mission accomplishment.

The management style communicated by the leaders of a new venture creates the culture in which day-to-day activities occur. Some cultures are supportive of the various internal stakeholders' values, beliefs and activities; other cultures may frustrate these stakeholders. While new venture managers can hire people who agree with the venture's mission and vision, it is more difficult to identify and hire people that will accept the culture. This is because the culture of a new venture is emerging; it is changing as the venture evolves from a small business run by one or two people to an enterprise that employs dozens and then hundreds. The way it feels inside the venture changes as the office (or plant) is expanded, as new people are hired and as more of the active external stakeholders are satisfied. The active internal stakeholders want a say in creating this evolving culture—they do not want to only be a consumer or recipient of the culture.

Passive External Stakeholders.   The passive external stakeholders include regulators, local governments, technology providers, journalists, business analysts and consumer interest groups. Because these stakeholders are both passive and external, they are most interested in knowing where the business is going—its destination. While they may not know the venture's vision or objectives, they will be aware of its mission, as this can often be interpreted from the venture's actions. If they accept this mission, they tend to remain passive. The services and ideas of these stakeholders may be solicited when needed; otherwise, they rarely try to influence the venture's activities.

If the passive external stakeholders do not accept the venture's mission or if they believe that the venture's actions are inconsistent with the mission and vision espoused, they may become active in their efforts to influence the venture's activities. Such attempts will generally be perceived by the new venture manager as hostile, obstructive or as efforts to block the venture's actions.

Passive Internal Stakeholders. Passive internal stakeholders—staff workers and the less skilled portions of the labor force—are not highly interested in or necessarily committed to the new venture. These stakeholders devote their attention to performing their assigned tasks and experiencing the climate and culture within which they work. While some individuals may be interested in the venture's course and destination, they are not likely to try to influence it in any strong way.

If the work environment meets their needs and the venture's activities do not violate their values or sense of equity, they will remain passive stakeholders. When their work environment needs are not being met, they may try to influence the venture, or more commonly, they choose to leave (subject to a healthy labor market for their skills).

MANAGING CHANGE

Having spent considerable time understanding who are the venture's stakeholders and what do they want—particularly the wants of the more active stakeholders—we must consider the effects of venture changes on these stakeholders. Figure 7.5 suggests that over time the venture will make significant changes in the way it conducts business, including new products, new target customers, new distribution channels, new employees and so on.

For some people, the relative stake that they have in the venture is not altered by these ongoing changes (signified by the letters A and D in Figure 7.5). Other relationships or stakeholder wants will be different after a change (noted by letters B and C). Which stakeholders and which stakeholder wants are changing is not always easy to diagnose while it is occurring. After the fact, it is often too late.

This has happened to many ventures that have expanded their business activities into unrelated products, altered substantially their distribution channels or expanded into a different geographical area. Brookstone is a successful New England merchandiser of hard-to-find hand tools. When a West Coast version of Brookstone was attempted, it ran into difficulty. While the first store opened was a success, the next three failed. The original

Figure 7.5   Stakeholders Often Change as the Venture Changes

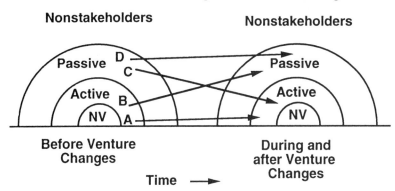

owners finally disposed of the venture. Their business plan was incomplete. They had failed to reassess their stakeholders in light of the changed locations—both from the East Coast to the West Coast and within California directly.

BUILDING THE BUSINESS

In Part I, we focused on an analysis framework for organizing our thoughts about a new venture—the 4-Box Model. In Part II, we have examined the elements of this analysis framework as they relate to building the business. Our focus has been on creating a shared sense of direction and identifying, influencing and embracing stakeholders. In Part III, we will shift our focus from analyzing and planning business initiatives to the internal management and leadership dynamics of a rapidly growing firm.

Part Three

■────────────────────────────────■

Thrust or Drift into the Next Decade?

T he mortality of small firms suggests that most enterprises (90 percent) do not reach the sweet spot of increasing sales and profit. Yet, 80 percent of the new ideas for products or services that led to the creation of a business that survives the start-up period are in existence ten or more years later. How can this be?

While most firms do not reach the sweet spot, their product or service survives in the marketplace because it is offered by a firm that does reach the sweet spot. The challenge for new venture managers is to successfully navigate through the rapid-growth period to become a force in the market.

Thus, new venture managers must both lead (do the *right things*) and manage (do *things right*). The natural tension between these two roles often results in one role dominating the other. When the leader role dominates, the venture grows out of control, first threatening its profitability and finally its survival. When the manager role dominates, control stifles growth, first threatening the venture's culture and finally its people, who withdraw and are replaced by the less competent. The venture prematurely matures and then declines, never attaining its desired sweet spot.

What is needed is an appropriate blend of growth, control and profits for each segment of a venture's development as it goes through its life-cycle. An imbalance of growth, control or profits prevents a new venture from reaching its potential. The venture's emerging structure, processes and procedures can either facilitate or impede its progress.

Many staff functions become necessary during the expansion stage—namely, recruiting, selection, compensation practices, legal services, data processing, accounting, financial management and information systems. These too can either facilitate or impede the venture's progress. The fact that these functions are handled by the new venture manager or consultants during start-up obfuscates the situation as the demand for these services increases during expansion.

New ventures experience *growing pains* during expansion. Some employees (including new venture managers) feel that there are not enough hours in the day to get the work done. "If the job is to be done right, I have to do it myself" is the battle cry. Others complain that they spend all of their time putting out fires, going to meetings or planning things rather than doing their real jobs.

There seems to be a scarcity of good managers—and no one knows how to identify and hire a "good manager." Yet some people are hired as managers nonetheless, and others are moved into management positions from within. Expansion leads to confusion about what various new people are doing as well as to a dilution of the shared understanding of where the firm is headed. The venture may continue to grow, but profits sag. Or profits are high, signifying short-term success. This is often followed by aggressive competitors attacking the "all too lucrative" market, leading to an eventual decline in the venture's market share due to a failure to reinvest in the distinctive competency of the business so as to keep it really distinctive.

New venture managers rarely have the time, knowledge and skills to be both efficient managers and effective leaders of all of the venture's activities alone. Many more people are hired during expansion, and this compounds the growing pains the venture is already experiencing. The venture develops a middle, with the associated challenges of middle-level employees acting as both leaders and followers. A more formal organizational structure with policies and standardized operating procedures emerges. But is anyone sure about which leadership and management structures, policies and procedures will support continued expansion? These are the topics to which Part III is devoted.

During the rapid-growth phase of the venture's life-cycle, the new venture manager can be compared to the owner of an 18-foot motorboat who is now the captain of a 150-foot ship. To make matters more difficult, the 150-foot ship is on its maiden voyage and does not have a complete set of blueprints and operating instructions. The sea is unfamiliar to the captain, and a storm is on the horizon.

The captain learns by *thinking, feeling* and *doing* collectively, at about the same time. This knowledge needs to be communicated efficiently to the crew—new knowledge not quickly transferred to the key workers means wasted resources and/or failure. Chapter 8 focuses on the ideas and concepts that are essential tools for the captain and crew. Developing skills as both a leader and manager are essential.

Ways to develop a shared understanding of the direction of the business among all employees and creating a corporate culture that empowers employees are discussed in chapter 9 so that you can overcome the 5 to 1 odds against reaching the sweet spot. Building trust, forming diagonal-slice groups, establishing a collateral organization and using self-directed teams are techniques to empower others. This is the true challenge of being both a manager and a leader.

Trust involves the sharing of information, influence and control. Rapid growth often leads to lower levels of trust among the organizational members. This must be overcome for the business to sustain its growth rate.

Diagonal-slice groups and collateral organizations are techniques for forming and using groups to address new venture issues that are not well handled by the existing organizational structure.

Self-directed work teams are groups of employees (generally four or more) that are responsible for a whole product, activity or process. The team plans the work and performs it, handling many of the things a manager might do and providing itself with leadership. Self-directed work teams, if designed and developed appropriately, become microentrepreneurial units. They facilitate the communication of the new venture manager's values and vision throughout their membership. By handling many of a manager's tasks within the group, fewer managers and less staff support is needed.

The final chapter, chapter 10, poses the ultimate challenge for a venture: to use its ideas to create a learning venture. Key ideas shared are reviewed in the context of five disciplines for achieving greatness.

8

───────────────────────────────

Learning, Leading
and Managing

It is frequently thought that successful new venture managers are different than other people and that they have particular background or personality characteristics that lead to their success. Researchers have tried to isolate these differences so as to help organizations select people who are more likely to be effective new venture managers.

This research has not led to many useful results. What we do know is that people who pursue entrepreneurial careers have many new venture failures along the way. Entrepreneurial skill may be learned, but is trial and error the only learning mechanism?

This chapter is organized into three sections. The first section discusses the ways in which we learn. Successful new venture managers, like many driven people, learn what is relevant to a business quickly and update that information often. To them, life is an ongoing learning process. They may not always be able to articulate what they have learned, but they can use it in their businesses.

The second section explores two responsibilities that must be assumed for a new venture to grow rapidly and profitably: (1) leadership and (2) management. The early success of a venture is based on the viability of the initial business proposition—either in the form of a business plan or simply a proposition that is carried around in the venture manager's head. Enough of the key success factors of the venture have been addressed or the venture would have failed.

This suggests that many of the key elements in the 4-Box Model are incorporated into the way a venture functions. These elements reflect the management side of a venture. The leadership side was discussed in Part II, "Building the Business." What is needed now is the integration of leading and managing.

The third section of this chapter examines the specific skills that are exhibited by successful managers and leaders. These skills are often sought and observed in high-performing organizations. The management skills reflect the areas of performance assessed on many performance appraisal forms across many lines of business. The leadership skills are those that have been observed in the more successful new ventures. Again, both sets of skills are needed for a new venture to reach its desired sweet spot.

THE WAYS WE LEARN

People are exposed to thousands of learning opportunities each day. As we experience these opportunities, we are simultaneously making implicit, often unconscious choices as to what we learn and how we learn it. In the American culture, the most accepted way of learning is through thinking— we experience life and think of things in various ways. Most of our educational system is based on such cognitive learning, and most of our social discussions rely on the expression of these thoughtful understandings to others. We are encouraged to share our ideas on business, people, various situations and events. Over two-thirds of our discussions focus on things that were learned primarily through our thought processes.

A second type of learning occurs via our emotions—we have feelings about something or someone. We may think about our feelings to understand them, but this does not mean that the learning takes place through thoughts. We can and do learn from our feelings.

Developing empathy for a customer may have little to do with our thoughts about the customer. The emotions felt from meeting and working with customers are the learning stimulus. We may rationalize these emotions through thoughts, but the learning is carried in the emotions. It is only when our emotions dominate our thoughts that the power of emotional learning is clear to us. What did it feel like the last time you laughed so hard that tears came to your eyes? What did it feel like when you experienced a tragedy—someone was hurt, died or was found to have a serious illness? Or when you felt exhilarated—at the top of the ski slope, in the middle of a business discussion or when selling someone on a great idea? Emotional learning is different from cognitive learning. Fortunately, they complement each other much of the time.

A third way in which we learn is through our actions. We do something, experience the result and have the opportunity to learn from that result. Again, we may think about it and feel something with respect to the experience, but here the learning occurs as a result of our actions and the feedback received from doing something. No one has ever learned to be a great performer by reading about it or by vicariously experiencing a great performance. These stimuli often provide the motivation or inspiration to pursue something; they do not provide the skill to perform at high levels.

It is through doing things that skill learning takes place. Some call this "practice." Others simply think of it as performing. Piano players play the piano for many hours before they perform on stage in front of others. So do baseball players and many other professionals. New venture managers rarely get the luxury of a practice session before each day of work. *Their work is their practice field as well as their performance field.*

What new venture managers need most in their quest for the sweet spot is to integrate the ways in which they learn into key insights and rules of thumb. They need a balance of cognitive, emotional and action-based learning so that each mode of learning compensates for the other mode's weaknesses.

- Overreliance on cognitive learning (often thought of as book learning or listening to the ideas of others, including consultants) leads to some great ideas that don't work in a particular situation.

- Overreliance on emotional learning (often thought of as soft, not analytic and overly concerned about how others feel) leads to inefficiencies, frustrations and staff dissatisfaction.

- Overreliance on action-based learning (often thought of as the ready, fire, aim approach) is costly. Trial-and-error learning can be expensive, and practice takes time and energy.

How do we integrate our thoughts, emotions and behaviors into a balanced learning approach? If we are able to do so, we can use the knowledge acquired each day as a foundation and springboard for continued success.

Intuition and Heuristics

Intuition is the ability to see the patterns and possibilities in a set of events. It allows one to see the forest as well as the trees. With intuition, one can see the emerging trend as well as the discrete data points that were collected to identify trends. Intuition, sometimes discussed as the sixth sense, is the ability to go beyond the immediate data to what is possible, given the data at hand.

The natural learning that our intuition creates is often turned into heuristics to guide our actions. A *heuristic* is a rule of thumb or a "soft rule"—something that guides us without controlling us. Managers develop hundreds of soft rules, many of which they use to guide their ventures. Some of these soft rules are sufficiently insightful and useful to advance a venture's growth and profits. But which ones?

New venture managers are not always conscious of the heuristics they are using, but a soft rule is operating nonetheless. Soft rules are learned ways of doing things that often provide effective guidance. Consider the following soft rules that people use each day:

- *Crossing a street.* Some people follow the rules established by traffic authorities (i.e., following the "walk" and "don't walk" signs), but others look, estimate and respond based on their estimates.

- *Interviewing a prospective employee.* Do you follow a structured interview process, using the same questions and evaluating the responses in the same way each time? Or do you have a general sense of the questions to ask and responses to expect? Each interview evolves a bit differently than previous interviews. Yet, you believe that you can make reliable and valid comparisons and judgments about the candidates.

- *Making a cup of coffee.* If you do not accurately measure out the water and coffee grounds each time, you have evolved a heuristic for the task. If you make great coffee each time, you have developed a rigorous heuristic. If your coffee is not so good, maybe some experimenting and rule making is in order.

- *Making a sales call.* The instruction one receives (if any) to make a sales call is a small part of a successful salesperson's understanding of what it takes to sell a product or service. Through a discovery process, new sales personnel begin to learn the task by doing it, thinking about what they are doing and becoming aware of how they feel about what they have done.

The heuristics new venture managers learn and apply are the essence of their running the venture. These heuristics are *not* rules, at least not hard rules. Rules are easy to write down, teach others and mechanically follow. The manager in each of us likes to turn soft rules into hard rules. The leader in us likes to inspire others to become familiar with the soft rules so as to use them appropriately more often.

Leadership implies an ongoing role of providing direction, inspiration and vision. Management involves creating systems, procedures and policies to perpetuate what has been learned. Both are needed; neither substitutes for the other.

As the previous examples suggest, people evolve soft rules for many of the activities that occur with some frequency in their lives (including lovemaking!). You certainly are not thinking about all the details surrounding an activity each time you do it. This requires too much of your energy, leaving too little energy for new tasks that require active learning. So you develop patterns of learned responses—some of which are rigorous heuristics that guide your behaviors, your attention and the venture.

Determining Your Soft Rules

There are many benefits to staying tuned-in to your natural discovery processes. First, you can access some of the insights you have had on a subconscious level that relate to the various things you do. Once these insights reach the conscious level, you can employ them more often when you see it as appropriate.

Second, you can use your knowledge of your patterned behaviors to diagnose your talents more accurately. If some things come naturally for you, look for more places where they are appropriate.

Third, you can create a development plan to alter those heuristics that are not effective so that you become more effective. If you make lousy coffee, whether or not you measure anything in the process, it may be time to try a new process. Or if you fall prey to exaggeration, often undermining your exaggerated point to those you are trying to influence, you may decide not to exaggerate—understatement may be your most powerful weapon.

Consider the following questions to diagnose your rigorous heuristics:

- What patterns of behavior do you have at work?

- For hiring people?

- For conducting meetings?

- For determining when to visit clients or key customers?

- For hiring temporary help?

- For taking risks?

- For seeking more capital?

- For reviewing orders, accounting information or market research?

- For dealing with conflict among employees?

- For handling customer complaints?

- Where have you evolved a structured way of thinking about a task, person or situation that "kicks in" every time that task, person or situation occurs?

- What are the key tasks you perform each day?

- What are your standard approaches, habits and operating procedures for these tasks?

- Are the heuristics you invoke for the above tasks rigorous?

- Do they work most of the time?

- When do they fail?

- When do they inhibit you?

Exploring your natural knowledge does not mean that this knowledge will or should remain constant for the life of the venture. Successful new venture managers find that their heuristics evolve; they become more refined and rigorous as the business grows. As the following example suggests, heuristics change as the venture attains rapid growth.

A Corona Beer Wholesaler

"When I first agreed to carry Corona Beer, I would order from the distributor (who then ordered from the brewery) the number of cases requested by my retailers. I was not sure of the actual consumer demand for Corona, as it was a Mexican beer that was fairly new to the States. The demand for it appeared to be erratic based on the orders I received from retailers (mostly convenience stores, bars and restaurants). So my orders to the distributor were erratic: 20 cases one week, 50 the next, none for three weeks, then 70 following that and so on.

"As I continued to carry Corona, I began to learn something about how these orders were both placed with me by my retailers and filled by the distributor. I wanted to get direct information on consumer interest in the product so I asked my drivers to survey the bartenders they knew best about the actual demand for Corona. I learned that demand was fairly predictable and increasing. I also learned that my distributor was second-guessing my orders and thereby was not always able to fill them completely.

"Rather than play a guessing game, I placed a standard order for Corona—50 cases the first week, 52 the second, 54 the third and so on for three months. I committed to these orders based on my understanding of consumer interest. After discussing this with my distributor, he agreed to meet my orders first, thereby reducing my stock outages but increasing my inventory of Corona if it did not move.

"The first two months were a bit testy. I had 140 cases on hand at one point and was expecting a delivery of 64 cases in two days. Then my intuition paid off. Several retailers in the area who were working through other wholesalers were out of stock—two weeks running. I was able to supply them Corona, reduce my inventory and maintain a great relationship with the distributor. Within five months, my weekly order was 100 cases—all of which were moving. There was a 100 percent increase in five months. While I hoped that this would continue, I had a feeling that it might not. Based on some feedback from my drivers and the retailers, I decided to hold my order constant at 104 cases per week—which I negotiated with the distributor.

"It is hard to tell whether I was smart or lucky. But the growth of Corona retail sales had led several other wholesalers to carry it. This led to greater retail availability and ultimately to a flattening of the demand for Corona *by the retailers that I served.* As Corona became an established beer within the States, I changed my approach entirely. I began to order it in proportion to the amount of other American beers ordered. I move about one case of Corona for every four cases of the leading American beer. I have been placing my orders in this ratio for about six months now, and it is working fine."

MANAGING *AND* LEADING

Up until a few years ago, the words *manager* and *leader* were used interchangeably by most people. We have discussed the role of a new venture manager—or is it new venture leader? What researchers and practitioners have found is that there are many skills that are needed to run an enterprise. Some of these skills have been discussed in the realm of management theory; others are more often discussed with respect to leadership theory. It is the new venture manager's challenge to both manage and lead.

In his book, *Mind of a Manager, Soul of a Leader* (Wiley, 1990), Craig Hickman shares 44 ways in which management and leadership are different. He proposes that there is a natural tension between managers and leaders and that you can tap that natural tension to your advantage by creating an environment that respects and empowers both of these roles within a business.

Some of the differences between management and leadership orientations that Hickman discusses are critical to the transition period that new ventures experience as they seek rapid growth. However, Hickman's book is directed at big businesses that have institutionalized management practices and hired so many managers that leadership is stifled. These businesses have taken the science of management too far. It is as if they are trying to create a technically correct musical score—one that meets all the principles of good music. This will not make a hit song, nor a song to which it is pleasant to listen.

In contrast to too much management and too many managers, new ventures that survive start-up have leadership—and they seek to develop some management practices (and managers) to complement their leadership strengths. But to become a "professionally managed organization" is *not* the solution.

The challenge is to integrate select management practices and a few managers into the rapidly growing venture. The key word here is *integrate*. The management and leadership orientations must be brought together.

Since the perspectives of managers differ from those of leaders, providing direction for these new managers is key. This is done through providing direction, direction and direction (as discussed in chapter 5). To integrate emerging managerial activities and new managers into the new venture, the leadership of the venture must provide clear and accepted direction as follows:

- *Direction as to the venture's destination*—sharing the venture's mission, vision and objectives

- *Direction as to the venture's heading and course*—identifying and following the venture's distinctive competence

- *Direction through the venture's management style*—creating a shared sense of values and an organizational culture that supports rapid, profitable growth

Direction as to the Venture's Destination

A management orientation to the mission, vision and objectives of a venture is to "lock them in" and "nail them down." Managers seek stability and dependability. They tend to be oriented toward short-term goals and focus on tangible results as proof of performance. Managers strive to conserve resources and compensate people for what it is they have done in the past. Their first acts as employees in a new venture are to reorganize business activities through greater division of labor and specialization, to refine inefficient practices and to develop compromises to eliminate observed conflicts among people. Their mind-set is to help the organization grow profitably through organizing, planning and controlling the work of others.

Most new venture managers are more adept at being leaders than managers. Their styles are different. While they recognize the value and need for management within the venture to sustain the rapid growth that the venture is experiencing, they see the venture's mission, vision and objectives as a sufficient organizing framework. As leaders, they accept and often seek change and independence. That is what the venture's reason for being is about—moving away from the past business activities and products their competitors offer into new, dynamic activities and products that they offer to better satisfy consumer wants.

New venture managers can envision a positive and successful business well into the future. They see the venture's potential, not just the measurable performance of last month. They can lead people by creating excitement

and making promises. Employee compensation tied to short-term performance may be necessary, but it is not sufficient to sustain growth. While not
against formal organizational structures and practices, new venture managers prefer to rethink activities and experiment with them. If the venture has
been flexible and fluid up until now, it should have some flexibility as it
moves forward.

Both management and leadership orientations are needed. For the venture to be successful, the leader needs to obtain the complete understanding
and acceptance of the venture's mission, vision and objectives from its
managers. Within this mission, vision and set of objectives, managers must
be empowered to apply their managerial skills—obtaining the organizational stability and product dependability that the science of management
can foster.

Direction as to the Venture's Heading and Course

A management orientation to the venture's distinctive competence is to
isolate it, protect it and target it to those markets that are supportive of that
distinctive competence. If changes are made that affect this competency,
these changes are done incrementally. This minimizes business risk and
reduces the likelihood that competitors and rivals will become aware of the
venture's strategy. Managers focus their energies on finding solutions to
problems and overcoming weaknesses in the venture's distinctive competence.

A leadership orientation to the venture's distinctive competence is different. The new venture manager, as its leader, helped create the competence.
If one distinctive competence can be created, so can another. Leaders look
for relationships between the venture's current competence and possible
future competencies. Protecting the competence is not as important as
identifying the next distinctive competence that will further satisfy consumer wants. Leaders get excited about making sweeping changes that
shake up competition. Risk is not risk in the traditional financial sense—risk
is what it takes to seek opportunities. Leaders focus their energies on finding
new issues to address in order to develop an even stronger distinctive
competence in the future.

This is the area of greatest challenge to the new venture manager. While
enhancing the venture's distinctive competence, or changing it, is often
appealing to their leadership orientation, it is fatal to the enterprise. New
venture managers must ensure that their managers know and embrace the
venture's distinctive competence—even when their leadership is pushing

the venture into new areas. Consumers, suppliers, buyers and most of the key stakeholders in the business are better served in the short run by sustaining the existing distinctive competence. Their immediate support is critical for rapid growth as the time and resources required to embrace new stakeholders ranges from months to years.

While new venture managers may choose to develop a different distinctive competence and work with a different set of stakeholders, this effort is best done as a venture within the venture. It is best to separate this activity from the prime venture as much as is possible—different people, facilities, budgets. This is what Apple Computer did when it decided to pursue the Macintosh line of computers. Over time, the Macintosh line has replaced most of the Apple line, but it was the growth in the Apple line that provided revenues in support of the Macintosh start-up.

Direction Through the Venture's Management Style

Probably the greatest differences between the management and leadership orientations are in the areas of values and culture. *Values* are those things that we hold dear to ourselves. Providing me with something that I value will yield substantial appreciation. Providing me with something that I do *not* value will go unacknowledged and unrewarded or may even receive criticism. Consider the following differences in what is valued by management and leadership:

Management Orientation Values	*Leadership Orientation Values*
analytical thinking	visionary thinking
hierarchy, power	cooperation, collaboration
taking charge	sharing accountabilities
skepticism	optimism
control	possibilities
scientific methods	artistic outcomes
authority	influence
standardization	agreement
instructions	inspiration
consistency	commitment
policy	shared folklore
measured results	movement toward vision

These different value orientations create two distinct cultures that have difficulty coexisting (but they must). The conflicts embedded in these cultures can add to the venture's problems, or they can be used as a point-counterpoint stimulus to challenge everyone's thinking. It is this dialectic discourse that improves the quality of decisions and thereby facilitates rapid growth and profitability.

If these two climates are left unattended, *the manager values will dominate the leader values.* Managers will gain increasing control over the venture, and new venture leaders will move on to other activities as they become disgruntled with the changes taking place that are creating a professionally managed firm. This occurs because the management orientation is more logical and provable than is the leadership orientation; it is also more conservative and predictable. These are the things that many of the venture's key stakeholders want. They require short-term results; in the long-term, they will all be dead, and they know it. Employees want job security, more pay and annual pay increases. Investors and partners want a return on their investments—in terms of dollars, equity and venture control.

The managers want the opportunity to do what it is they were hired to do—namely, turn the venture into a professionally managed firm. This means they will gain more influence and authority, creating structures to institutionalize the management methods that they have introduced and developing operating practices to eliminate human judgment whenever and wherever possible. In short, there are ample pressures to turn the venture into an efficient machine that is capable of doing the same thing, "the one best way," every time. But there is no one best way! There are many good ways, with the best way being undeterminable in all but the most static environments. The preferred way draws on the venture's strengths, remains flexible and responsive and is right for the moment.

Where Does Your Venture Stand?

While management and managers are needed, they are often employed beyond the real needs of the venture during its early growth stage. Until the sweet spot is reached, it is better to err on the side of too much leadership than too much management. Both are needed but to a different extent at different stages in the growth cycle. During rapid growth, lead first, manage second.

Consider the following questions as you assess the relative amount of leadership and management now occurring within your venture. *Is an appropriate balance being maintained between the management and leadership orientations?*

- Is our approach to consumer needs balanced?

- Where are we managing these relationships? Where are we leading them?

- Are we fulfilling current consumer needs as well as exploring how to satisfy their emerging needs?

- Are we mechanistic in our approach to satisfying consumer needs?

- How is this received by our customers?

- Is our understanding of competitors' strengths and weaknesses based on sound analyses?

- Is that understanding augmented by our sense of their vision for themselves?

- Is it augmented by our sense of trends in the industry?

- What are our competitors' emerging strengths? Weaknesses?

- What trends are affecting our business?

- How are we benefiting by these trends?

- Are we examining the environment for new trends?

- What new trends have been found?

- Are the business profit and loss *dynamics* known to all employees?

- Are these dynamics changing?

- Do our goals and objectives provide direction to the people who can affect goal outcomes?

- Are our goals and objectives constraining the useful initiatives of key employees?

- Do we have an accurate understanding of our strengths? Problems? Opportunities? Threats?

- Is our distinctive competence solid?

- Can it be improved?

- Is our distinctive competence known to newer employees?

- Are our target markets outperforming nontargeted markets?

- Are there additional target markets we should be serving?

- Is our positioning the desired positioning for the future? If not, what is being done to alter it?

- Is the venture's distinctive competence clear within our positioning?

- Are our products right for today, yesterday or tomorrow?

- Is our pricing right for today, yesterday or tomorrow?

- Are the distribution channels performing as expected? To the desired capacity?

- Have alternative channels of distribution become accepted within the industry? Are we using them?

- Are our promotions leading to the desired short-term results?

- Do our promotions still have vitality?

- Are the relevant people being informed of key changes in the business?

- Who are these people?

- Who is keeping them informed?

- Do new employees understand and share the venture's vision? How do you know?

- Are managers extending our sense of direction to their subordinates? How do you know?

- Are our programs leading to the desired results?

- How can we extend these results?

- Is our MIS linked to changes in our profit-loss dynamics? Prove it to yourself.

- Is our research driven by the need to reduce decisional risk?

- What do we do differently based on our research results?

- What benefits have we accrued from our research in the last two months?

As you reflect on these questions, ask yourself what is being nailed down and what is being made more efficient and cost-effective for the business.

For profitable rapid growth, some things need to be nailed down. They need to be managed. Other things need to be expanded, altered, experimented with and given a chance to succeed or fail. These latter things need to be led.

THE SKILLS OF A MANAGER, THE SKILLS OF A LEADER

The third area to explore within the venture is the extent to which the necessary skills are present and exercised by the venture's employees. These skills are distinct from how the venture learns and its management and leadership orientation.

The distinct nature of skills occurred to me one day on a walk through the Soho area of New York City. Having glanced into the cellar of a factory,

I saw a person building a coffee table. As I moved on, I reflected on my abilities to do what I saw being done. My dad had built the coffee table that was in our living room for most of my childhood.

I had most of the same tools as my dad and the carpenter I observed that day, and I could acquire critical table parts. I knew what steps had to be taken. I knew what the finished product looked like. So why did I feel that I could not do as good a job as the person I just watched? What I lacked was the skill—that learned ability to do a thing competently with style, efficiency and effectiveness.

Management Skills

Managerial skills have been the topics of research and practice for nearly one hundred years. While the list of skills keeps getting longer, there are nine areas of competency that are accepted by researchers and managers alike as being important to human performance in work organizations. Managers need skills in the following nine areas:

1. Setting objectives and establishing priorities

2. Clarifying relationships and needed actions

3. Relying appropriately on hierarchy

4. Distributing information and delegating tasks

5. Involving or representing relevant others

6. Motivating others to perform at high levels

7. Facilitating interaction and communicating effectively

8. Taking appropriate action on priority issues

9. Developing, evolving, sharing strategy

How do you see your managerial skill level? As you review the behaviors that follow, reflect on various meetings, interactions or situations that have required managerial skill. Then circle a response based on this scale:

1 = This behavior is *exhibited effectively;* no improvement is needed.

2 = This behavior is *adequate;* some improvement is desired.

3 = *Development is needed.*

Do I:	Exhibited Effectively	Adequate	Development Needed
1. *Set* realistic and challenging *objectives?*	1	2	3
2. *Establish priorities* regarding what and when something is to be done?	1	2	3
3. Discuss shared problems with relevant others to *get needed actions started?*	1	2	3
4. *Get issue clarity* through establishing an agenda at meetings?	1	2	3
5. *Rely on hierarchy* to provide direction?	1	2	3
6. *Show respect for hierarchical position?*	1	2	3
7. *Distribute information* to others that is relevant to their work?	1	2	3
8. *Delegate tasks* to appropriate others, identifying the need for actions and time for feedback?	1	2	3
9. *Involve others* who are affected by an issue?	1	2	3
10. *Represent* the interests of subordinates to influential others?	1	2	3
11. *Motivate others* to perform at high levels?	1	2	3
12. *Stimulate enthusiasm* for work activities?	1	2	3

13. *Interact with many others,* asking questions and encouraging them to share ideas or information?	1	2	3
14. *Communicate* in a concise, convincing manner?	1	2	3
15. *Seek alternative views* until a decision is made?	1	2	3
16. *Remain open* to alternative courses of action as new opportunities or threats are disclosed?	1	2	3
17. *Articulate a conceptual understanding* of what the business unit is attempting to do?	1	2	3
18. Clearly *understand our distinctive competence* and actively manage to enhance it?	1	2	3
19. *Manage effectively,* achieving the results desired by management?	1	2	3
20. *Facilitate the performance and development* of associates and/or subordinates?	1	2	3

Leadership Skills

A second and distinct set of qualities differentiates people seen as effective in their leadership efforts and those viewed as needing development in this area. Research that supports these skills is reported in *Taking Charge: Strategic Leadership in the Middle Game,* by Stephen A. Stumpf and Thomas P. Mullen (Prentice-Hall, 1992). Leadership skills involve a manager's ability to

1. know the business and markets,

2. manage subunit rivalry,

3. find and overcome threats,

4. stay on strategy,

5. be an entrepreneurial force and

6. accommodate adversity.

This set of strategic management skills differentiates the apprentice manager from the craftsperson leader. While exhibiting managerial competencies will help one to reach a management position, being effective in leading a new venture demands further skills. Most managers have not had a chance to develop these skills because their organizations are not clear on the need for them and the demands and hectic pace of their jobs leaves little time for them to acquire these skills along the way.

How do you see your leadership skill level? As you review the items listed below, reflect on various meetings or discussions that have involved strategic issues. Then circle a response based on the following scale:

1 = This behavior is *exhibited effectively;* no improvement is needed.

2 = This behavior is *adequate;* some improvement is desired.

3 = *Development is needed.*

Do I:	*Exhibited Effectively*	*Adequate*	*Development Needed*
Know the Business and Markets?			
1. Actively consider what product and service features consumers or users want?	1	2	3
2. Identify and interpret social, economic and political trends that could affect the business?	1	2	3

3. Articulate a conceptual understanding of the venture's past actions?   1   2   3

4. Ask thought-provoking questions that relate to the venture's future actions?   1   2   3

5. Generate many alternatives to key issues—for example, by answering "what if" questions?   1   2   3

Manage Subunit Rivalry?

6. Establish and communicate venture objectives?   1   2   3

7. Foster crossfunctional communications?   1   2   3

8. Manage crossfunctional relationships effectively?   1   2   3

Find and Overcome Threats?

9. Quickly spot problems and address their broader implications?   1   2   3

10. Redefine issues to make them more understandable?   1   2   3

11. Identify constraints to remove or avoid them?   1   2   3

Stay on Strategy?

12. Capitalize on the venture's strengths?   1   2   3

13. Seek to strengthen the venture's competitive advantage?   1   2   3

14. Focus on specific target markets?	1	2	3

Act as an Entrepreneurial Force?

15. Create a vision of what the venture could be?	1	2	3
16. Champion innovative ideas, even when faced with skepticism, risk and/or resistance?	1	2	3
17. Influence and excite others to take desired actions?	1	2	3

Accommodate Adversity Well?

18. Respond flexibly to problems, opportunities and threats?	1	2	3
19. Exhibit comfort and tolerance when dealing with ambiguous tasks?	1	2	3
20. Deal with setbacks by being resilient?	1	2	3

It is through these managerial and leadership skills that the mission, vision and objectives of the venture are enacted. While the specific issues pertinent to each venture differ, the skills needed to address the issues in a productive manner are similar.

SELF-ASSESSMENT SUMMARY—SPOT

The concept of a SPOT analysis was suggested in chapter 2 as a way to summarize the current business situation. (It is reprinted in Figure 8.1.) By developing a detailed understanding of the business's strengths, problems, opportunities and threats, it is possible to develop alternative courses of action to best leverage the business situation.

SPOT is an equally valuable tool to summarize your current management-leadership situation.

- What are your strengths?

- Based on the self-assessment you just conducted, what do you do particularly well?

- What are your problems (or weaknesses)?

- Where is development needed?

- What opportunities exist for you to leverage your strengths or develop your weaknesses?

- What threats may materialize if you do not leverage your strengths or develop your weaknesses?

By summarizing your personal situation using SPOT, you will have (on a single page) a profile of your situation that can guide future activities.

The assessments made in this chapter need not be yours alone. Who else in the venture should be answering these same questions? Obtaining a second or third perspective on the situation can be valuable in several ways. If it confirms your views, this provides you with a sense of confidence in your perceptions. If others have different views, you have the opportunity to discuss their views and evolve a common view on which to proceed.

Building a shared vision of the future involves working through the various perspectives of key stakeholders. While this takes time and patience with the process, it is a better use of your time than putting out all the fires that are started due to a lack of shared vision. Summarize your perspective on the SPOT chart in Figure 8.1. Share it with significant others. Work toward a mutual understanding that can be used as the foundation for future business decisions.

Figure 8.1   SPOT Chart for Analyzing Your Leadership Situation

Strengths
What do I do well now?

Problems
What gaps exist between where I am now and where I expected to be?

Opportunities
What possibilities exist?

Threats
What can go wrong?

9

Empowering Others To Overcome the Odds

Eighteen highly successful new venture managers who were serving on the advisory board of an entrepreneurship research center associated with a major university were asked, "If you could mention only one thing that made the difference, that kept the venture moving toward that sweet spot, what was it?" They each wrote their answer down before disclosing it to the group. Fourteen of them answered "the people they worked with." Three others said "getting the work done and problems solved through their people."

In the discussion that followed, the new venture managers were quick to add the importance of satisfying customer needs, obtaining funding, developing relationships with members of the distribution channel and having a high-quality product to offer.

To understand their initial answers, we asked, "Why are the people the most critical resource?" Many answers were given, from "you can't do it all yourself" to "many hands make light work" to "growth can only occur, beyond some initial success, through expansion—people are always needed for that." The answer that received the greatest support from these managers was given by the leader of a highly successful medical products company: "The venture needs a lot of things to grow rapidly, and a lot of skills to grow profitably. Most things you need, you can get. And when you get them, they stay got. People are different. They need to be changing as rapidly as the venture is changing—some grow with it; others don't. Some grow in different directions than you expected, or sometimes wanted. Attending to the people issues is never-ending, not for a day, not for an hour.

"When I hired someone to manage the expansion, the investment of my time and attention was ongoing. The person I hired was great, but ongoing leadership was still needed."

If people are the most critical resource needed to grow a new venture rapidly and profitably, how does each venture manager effectively manage and lead many people? Our discussion of the human aspect of a venture began in Part II, "Building the Business." We explored the importance of providing people with direction and identifying and influencing stakeholders; we brought the human side of enterprise into the new venture growth process. The discussion of this "people" component continued in chapter 8 ("Learning, Leading *and* Managing"), which focused on what new venture managers do personally to learn, to lead and to manage people.

To go beyond effective self-management, we need to tap the potential of the venture's many internal stakeholders. Some of these stakeholders must become empowered to make decisions and take actions in support of the venture's mission, vision and objectives. Exploring how you can make this happen is the focus of this chapter.

People become empowered in many ways. One way is to link their activities and decisions to the direct power and authority of the new venture manager. If the boss gives them the authority to do something (often through delegation), then they are empowered to act.

When a venture is small and there are few employees, delegation is an efficient way to empower people. It keeps the venture's control close to the new venture manager up until the time the venture manager chooses to empower others to handle specific issues. *Delegation with control is a management skill that empowers others to act on specific tasks as agreed to in the delegation episode.*

Survival and venture growth has made empowerment through delegation and personal contact with the new venture manager somewhat inefficient. The breadth and number of activities in which the venture is involved are more than one person can fully understand, no less control. If the new venture manager is not available when new issues arise, things do not get done. Additional means of empowering people are necessary. The most pervasive means of empowering people is through the venture's culture.

EMPOWERING PEOPLE THROUGH A
VENTURE'S CULTURE

When a new venture starts, it has no culture, as it has no history. Culture is embedded in the history of a society or company.

As a venture survives start-up, it begins to evolve a culture—one that is heavily influenced by the new venture manager *and* the broader environment in which the venture functions. New venture managers bring their values, style and vision to the culture. The environment brings industry, competitor practices, consumers, suppliers and buyers to the culture.

A venture's culture becomes a blend of the new venture manager and the environment. It can be observed in those rather repetitive ways by which the venture's members seem to get things done. As you describe these "habits," you are characterizing the venture's culture.

While organizational culture is an abstract concept, its power is concrete. *It is the venture's culture, more so than its managers, that leads employees to feel empowered during the rapid-growth period.* Since new venture managers are overwhelmed with business activity during rapid growth, they rarely devote sufficient time and energy to managing their people. It is possible for the culture that has been created to overcome some of this management inattention.

The venture's culture is a set of guidelines. Conforming to cultural norms facilitates getting things done. By knowing the culture, people can take actions that are consistent with that culture with less risk of criticism or resistance. Violating cultural norms often leads to problems or failures—both personally and organizationally. Consider the following statements new venture managers have made that reflect the cultural norms of their ventures two to three years after start-up:

- "If something is not working as it should, raise the issue with the new venture manager."

- "If you see something wrong, fix it."

- "If you have a problem with someone, try to avoid that person—work with someone else."

- "Talk through your differences—nobody has all the answers around here."

- "Things are so busy that you have to ask for things—what you don't ask for, you'll never get."

- "We 'stop the world' every few months to see where we are at. Resources get reallocated at that time to ensure that everyone is treated in a way that will continue their involvement and the venture's growth."

- "The equity partners have all the say. Everyone else is a worker."

- "I don't even know who the equity partners are; the people who have influence here are the ones that know how to get the job done."

- "Everything is a crisis. We spend much of our time solving problems and minimizing the pain."

- "Things are very exciting. There is never a dull moment."

- "Ready, fire, aim. I think that captures the way we approach things."

- "'If it is worth doing, it is worth doing right,' is our motto."

These statements describe how people are expected to behave within their respective ventures. Each of these aspects of the venture's culture says, "This is the way to do things." Implicit in each statement is "Go out and try it this way."

Each *pair of statements* represents opposite cultural norms—norms shared with me by people employed in different ventures. Knowing which norms apply in your venture is the difference between constructing an approach that is likely to be supported and one that is likely to be resisted. Conforming to cultural norms leads to empowerment—the ability to take actions without prior explicit approval. Violating cultural norms leads to being increasingly monitored and controlled.

To achieve rapid, profitable growth, the venture's employees need to diagnose and attend to the venture's cultural and operating norms. Since such norms focus on how to do things, rather than on what specific action to take, it is often necessary to adjust the means used to reflect the culture in order to accomplish the desired ends. It is the venture's culture that suggests answers to the "how" questions; the venture's mission, vision and objectives focus on the "what" questions.

While venture cultures vary along many attributes, there are some distinguishable patterns of habits and norms that create discrete cultures. At the risk of oversimplifying the complexity of issues that new venture managers confront, two cultures are described: (1) a person-centered culture and (2) a venture-centered culture. Both cultures empower people who conform to the culture to act. But the nature of the actions is quite different.

A Person-Centered Culture—Investcorp

Many new venture managers organize and run their businesses in whatever way they feel best reflects their personal interests and the skills and interests of their partners. By leveraging their specific strengths and those of their partners (and possibly other key internal stakeholders), they create a culture that reflects the values and operating procedures of these people. We refer to such a culture as *person-centered*—it is centered around specific persons (not necessarily people in general).

A small, five-year-old financial services company, Investcorp (fictitious name), has a person-centered culture. Investcorp does investment banking, trading and securities brokerage activities. Observations of people who work for Investcorp suggest that they

1. operate in an independent, autonomous manner;
2. tailor products and services to customer requests;
3. aggressively compete with other businesses that serve the same customers;
4. try to develop their general management skills rather than specific technical skills;
5. encourage creativity and innovation within their work force to best serve consumers and develop a competitive advantage;
6. provide rewards based on merit, using easily measured performance criteria (e.g., a closed deal);
7. promote the best talent available from within *or* hire from outside of the venture—whichever is easier at the time;
8. use expert consultants to develop solutions to problems;
9. treat people as if they are only as good as their last accomplishment; and
10. manage the venture to obtain immediate growth and short-term profitability.

If one puts aside any personal preferences for working within Investcorp's person-centered culture, then these attributes are neither good nor bad. They simply reflect the culture that emerged within Investcorp as a function of the mission, vision and objectives established by the new venture manager and the industry within which it competes.

The types of people who are recruited, hired and retained at Investcorp reflect this culture. They tend to be independent, aggressive and self-sufficient. Conflict among the professional employees over issues is openly accepted and often encouraged. This leads to creative solutions to many of the problems and challenges confronted. The "winner" of the conflict, as determined by the market, receives a commission consistent with the size of the deal.

The level of excitement, energy and intensity at Investcorp's offices is high. People come in early and stay late. If you are not working on several deals at the same time, you risk being labeled an "empty shirt." These are fast times in the financial services industry, and Investcorp wants to become a major player in the industry. Work hard, play hard and win is a fair description of Investcorp's culture. Get what you can before you burn out describes how many of the professional staff view their role in the venture.

People who join Investcorp quickly learn of this culture. In many cases, they are attracted to the investment banking industry and Investcorp because of its reputation for a person-centered culture. Newcomers know that they will be given extensive power to make deals happen—if they are successful, they will be well rewarded. If they cannot close the deals, they will not receive a commission or bonus and may have a relatively short tenure with the firm if their ability to close a deal does not change quickly. They also know that last year's successes are of little value this year. As soon as a deal is over, it is history. You get to keep the money, but the fame and power fade away rather quickly. There are few historians in investment banking firms.

Has Investcorp been successful with its person-centered culture? By most standards, the answer is yes. Many of its people are very successful; some have become quite rich.

Investcorp itself does not exist today. It was bought by a bigger securities brokerage firm last year. Some of its employees (and partners) have left to join other firms, some have left to create new firms of their own and others are now employees of the new parent company.

Does Investcorp's parent company have the same culture as Investcorp? To some extent, yes. It is in the same industry, and its founders were aggressive, independent types. But some of the aspects of Investcorp's culture that truly empowered Investcorp employees are less intense in the larger firm. For example, more permissions and approvals are needed for the bigger deals or for deals involving clients that are Fortune 500 firms.

This is to be expected since the older, larger firms in most industries are more bureaucratic than their younger, smaller counterparts. It is ironic that large firms often buy small firms for the smaller firm's ability to be aggressive in the market. Then they stifle that aggressiveness through a culture and management procedures that limit the power of those managers and professionals they really want to be aggressive.

A Venture-Centered Culture—InfoServe

An alternative to the person-centered culture is the culture that is collegial and team oriented. This type of culture supports the sharing of information and resources across functional and product lines. The focus of such a culture is on the venture, not on individuals per se. This kind of culture reinforces a venture's focus on customers or customer relationships instead of the specific and discrete products or services the customer uses or consumes.

Central to managing a venture-centered culture is for people to be able to solve problems and take initiatives that are in the best interest of the venture. This must be done even when people do *not*

1. have sole responsibility and accountability for their actions, and

2. necessarily perceive their actions as being in their personal, short-term best interest.

The culture must convince people to accept the efficacy of investing their efforts to accomplish venture goals, often trading off some individual goal accomplishment. This aspect of the culture is particularly important to reinforce because people may not always get personal acknowledgement for their positive contributions to attaining the venture's goals but will likely feel some blame for their lack of contribution to goals that are not accomplished.

A newspaper publishing company launched a new venture in the area of electronic information services. For the new venture (call it InfoServe) to be successful, the publisher and the new venture manager knew that it would be critical for the resources of the firm to be openly and efficiently shared across the business lines (journalism and information data base creation and sales). Consider the following ways in which InfoServe works to create and sustain a venture-centered culture:

• People are encouraged to operate in an interdependent, collaborative manner.

- The venture seeks to offer a uniform set of products and services to all markets, allowing the end user to customize the product as needed.

- Employees are expected to actively collaborate with other businesses within the company that serve the same customers.

- People within the venture develop a depth of knowledge in functional and technical areas so that, upon transfer, the successes in one area can be transferred to other areas.

- Management encourages consistency and excellence in execution within each market to effectively serve the consumer and develop a national competitive advantage.

- Rewards and promotions are based on loyalty and merit using subjective and objective performance criteria.

- The best talent available is transferred around the organization; outside resources are rarely used.

- Process consultants are used to facilitate discussion among parties in conflict.

- People are valued for their collective contributions to the business and for their ongoing personal development.

As with the person-centered culture, a venture-centered culture is neither good nor bad. The InfoServe culture is certainly different than the person-centered culture that emerged and was reinforced at Investcorp.

InfoServe's culture empowers people to work together, share information and conduct their activities so as to be of benefit to multiple areas of the organization. Personal development is valued as much as personal performance. Quality service and developing long-term customer relationships are more important than short-term individual contributions to the bottom line. Loyalty is valued more than "star" performance.

InfoServe's efforts to create and empower its people to behave according to venture-centered cultural norms have paid off; growth and profits have been substantial. Turnover is low; transfers between lines of business and across functional areas are the most common type of career move. Problems arise and are solved at InfoServe at whatever level experiences the problem. Higher levels of management are kept informed of problem solutions and of the status on any issues that have yet to be resolved.

As stated by one professional staff member, "We all are pretty clear on what we are trying to accomplish. We have several models from the marketplace of good data-base systems. We want to develop the best—in terms of content, easy access and currency. When something comes up that looks like it is going to undermine our efforts to accomplish this goal, we tackle it directly and quickly. Sometimes we screw up, but that's all part of the game."

Aspects of Cultures That Empower People

What is it about your venture's culture that is empowering people to do things that will lead to the accomplishment of key objectives? Consider the following questions as you reflect on the culture of your business activities:

- What patterns of behavior exist in the venture? In sales? In production? In office protocol?

- What happens when a new idea is proposed?

- How long does a new idea live before it is shot down or forgotten?

- How often do positive things get done that you only learn about after they are completed?

- Are the failures shared in an open and timely manner?

- Do the messengers get shot? Do they fear that they will?

- Is business activity team or individually focused?

- How many teams, task forces and groups are you part of within the venture? Your direct reports?

- Do employees take business risks without prior approval?

- How big are these risks?

- How are the people who are viewed as responsible for unsuccessful business risks handled?

- Is informal or social discussion viewed as work or a waste of time?

- Do people share their personal goals as well as their business goals with you? With each other?

- How many people are involved in most major decisions?

- How many more people might want to be involved if they were asked?

- Do people feel personally accountable for their contributions to the business?

- Are people energetic and motivated?

- Do they take initiative?

- Do people strive for excellence in all that they do?

- Do people actively seek control when unforeseen events happen?

- Do people feel so committed to the venture that they do *not* intend to leave?

TECHNIQUES USED TO EMPOWER OTHERS

With a charismatic, visionary leader and cultural norms that are supportive of empowering people to do the things the leader wants, a new venture can overcome the 5 to 1 odds against reaching the sweet spot. What if you believe you have these attributes, but rapid growth or profits are not forthcoming?

The ideas discussed earlier with respect to the 4-Box Model, direction and stakeholders may certainly provide some useful questions to answer. If your answers come back to people issues—getting your people to do more and to work better for the venture—then more empowerment is needed.

New ventures as well as established companies are challenged to find ways to empower employees. As organizations grow, they institute business practices that are intended to replace human judgment with standardized procedures—for example, for financial reporting, accounting, marketing and management. As these business practices take hold, people begin to give less of themselves to the business. They do what they are told or what they will be formally rewarded for doing. This leads to compliance, not empowerment.

To overcome this, several management techniques have been used to empower people to accomplish important venture goals. Four techniques are particularly relevant to new ventures. Each of these techniques—building trust, forming diagonal-slice groups, establishing a collateral organization and using self-directed teams—is discussed below as a way to empower people to get things done.

Building Trust

Trust is a set of beliefs about an interpersonal relationship that have crystallized over time based on your experiences with another person. Trust always involves others. You may say that you trust yourself, but you probably mean that you have confidence in yourself. Confidence in others can lead to trusting them more, but confidence is not trust.

To exhibit trust, you increase your vulnerability through another person. If you are not vulnerable, you are not really trusting someone. Vulnerability implies that there is a potential loss or penalty at stake if the other party does not protect your vulnerability. For example, you decide to lend someone your car. You trust that person to drive it safely and return without damage to the car, to others or to himself or herself. (For more information on trust, see Dale E. Zand, *Information, Organization, and Power: Effective Management in the Knowledge Society* [New York: McGraw Hill, 1981].)

When viewed in this way, trust is an important attribute of new venture activities and relationships. In just how many situations are you willing to become vulnerable to the extent that if your vulnerability is protected, you benefit a little; but if your vulnerability is not protected, you lose a lot?

This is like a biased gamble. I bet ten dollars; if I win, I get my ten dollars back plus two. If I lose, I lose the ten spot. I have to win five times to make up for every loss. To make such bets, I must believe that there is a better than 5 to 1 chance that my bet will win. If the odds are 5 to 1 or less, I will lose more than I ever win. Assuming I keep my wits about me, I would stop participating in any situation that had these attributes.

What Determines Trust?   If the goal is to build more trust into work relationships so as to empower people to act, we must know more about how trust is determined. Are some people more trusting than others? Sure. The most trusting people often are viewed as naive or gullible. People have a predisposition to trust (or not to trust) based on their upbringing, the results of past situations in which they have trusted others and training they have had related to building interpersonal relationships.

The competence that another person has for the task at hand will also contribute to whether or not you trust that person. You probably trust the accountant to do the books according to generally accepted accounting principles more than you trust your marketing manager to do the same task.

Trust becomes interesting when you do *not* have a specialist for a task. Who do you ask then, or do you do it yourself? Part of empowering others is to have them "step up to the plate" when something needs to be done that is new or different. No one may have the necessary competence—someone will learn it as that person works the issue through. The cost of this learning may be several failures or mistakes. *Who do you let make mistakes?* These are the people in whom you express the most trust.

Trust is enhanced when people are open with information—not just facts. They must be open with their ideas, judgments, intentions and feelings. This allows you to develop an understanding of their perspective and to develop your personal beliefs about their ability, intentions and objectives. By not exploiting this information, you reinforce the trust that is developing. By sharing similar information, you build a trust cycle, which encourages people to be more forthcoming with information in the future.

Effects of Trust and Mistrust. The benefits of trust are many—so many, in fact, that it is a bit irrational that we do not risk trusting people more often. With trust comes a greater openness and sharing of ideas. The ideas shared often involve greater creativity as people become less worried about negative criticism for suggesting something that is not a "perfect idea as first expressed."

In problem-solving situations, trust leads to greater exploration of alternative courses of action, more support for individual preferences and greater motivation to implement the decisions reached. People who trust each other are more inclined to work well together on team activities, and they express greater loyalty to the venture.

Mistrust not only eliminates these benefits of trust, but it disempowers people. Why take a risk if you will be blamed for the failure? If you wait until you are told to do something, then the blame can be shared with whoever provided the instructions. "I was just doing what I was told" is the most common excuse given in low-trust organizations.

Under conditions of mistrust, the uncertainty experienced in a situation increases. The higher the uncertainty, the less likely people are to take actions without overt permission because they "just didn't know what to do." So they do nothing. They do not want to be blamed for an action if it does not work out as expected.

Mistrust also leads to poor information exchange, as people protect what they know by not sharing it with others. Because information is not shared, there is less interpersonal influence among people. When was the last time you felt influenced by someone you did not trust? You may be controlled by someone you distrust because they also control the key resources (including your salary or position), but you rarely accept their interpersonal influence.

Expressing Trust.   To build trust within a venture, you must first express trust in others. While anyone can express trust, it is generally the senior-most people that start the trust-building cycle. One way to start is to become more open with what has traditionally been privy information. Now that the venture has survived, what kinds of information can be disclosed that you may have felt was too threatening or risky to share in the past?

A number of people have "hung in there" with you; if you want to begin building their trust, you will need to share more. Consider sharing with others the key facts, alternatives, judgments, intentions and feelings that are related to their area of business activity. When people get privy information from the boss that is germane to their activities, they feel privileged and empowered. They want to do something with this knowledge to show the boss that it has value to them.

A second way to express trust is to accept the goals, concepts, plans and suggestions of others. The risk in so doing is that they may want to do some things the venture is not prepared to support. How likely is this? Accepting a person's goals does not mean that the goals will be accomplished or that they will remain that person's goals over the long term.

Think of some of the goals you have had, of how often they change and of how they tend to evolve in response to outside events. To the extent that there is a shared sense of mission and vision for the venture, other people's goals, concepts, plans and suggestions are alternative ways to accomplish the same things. Their ideas may not be as good as yours, but they are more motivated to enact their ideas than they are to enact yours. Trust them. Empower them to act.

As the venture grows, there is the omnipresent feeling that things are getting out of control. There is a tendency to build control systems for everything. Once the hard-core managers take charge, things will be controlled whether they need to be or not.

Control drives out trust. Do *not* impose controls when only coordination is necessary. Are you seeking the energy, commitment and thinking of your employees or just their compliance?

Control breeds compliance. Are the venture's activities sufficiently stable and predictable that only compliance is needed? This implies that everything that needs to be done for growth and profitability can be articulated, communicated, enacted and measured. Is this the situation the venture now experiences?

Trust at Conrad Electronics. Conrad Electronics is a five-year-old venture. It designs and manufactures receivers, transmitters, amplifiers and other specialized electronic equipment. It sells its products in several markets, including sales to original equipment manufacturers, distributors who supply retailers and the government.

The company was profitable during its first three years, with 55 percent of its sales on a cost-plus basis to the government and various prime contractors. Then technology began to change; government purchases declined, and the company faced increasingly strong competition.

By the middle of the fourth year, the situation was viewed as severe. Sales volume was still increasing, but no profits were being made. Conrad ended its fourth year with a $367,000 loss. The board of directors met with the president after the annual meeting to inform him that he had two years to turn the situation around. He would be replaced at that time if Conrad was not comfortably in the black.

Under these circumstances the president tentatively concluded that modernization and expansion were not feasible. It would take more than a year to locate a new site, construct buildings, move equipment and people and arrange the necessary financing. Also the board probably would not approve a heavy capital program. If anything, these activities would interfere with productivity and decrease short-term profits.

Yet, the president believed that anything that he could squeeze out of the business over the next two years would only hurt the venture's longer-term growth. The president decided to meet with his vice-presidents to formulate appropriate plans.

The problems facing Conrad Electronics were critical and complex. Small improvements in the quality of management's decisions and small increases in the motivation of managers could have a great impact on results. The central problem required developing a strategy that would increase short-term profits without undermining long-term growth. This had to be done with support for short-term actions despite the likely disappointment of the vice-presidents over delays in the modernization and expansion that they wanted.

The specific actions taken turned out to be of much less importance than the trust that was created among the president and vice-presidents. Without truly understanding why, the president decided to disclose everything he knew about the situation, including the board's ultimatum. After the initial shock, the group began to brainstorm possibilities, share concerns, develop alternatives and formulate a strategy. They then took these ideas down to their people. A similar sharing of all of the facts followed, including the board's ultimatum.

Over the next six months, Conrad began to accomplish things that a year earlier would not have been considered. Managers reported a higher level of trust in each other and felt empowered to do their jobs in spite of a host of barriers that emerged. They broke even that year, negotiated for capital funds for the following year and turned the business around to a reasonable profit within two full years.

When asked about the situation, three of the five vice-presidents reported that they would have left the firm had the president not let them share in the problem. As one vice-president said, "To have a sizable loss one year and your budget cut the next would have been ample stimulus to go elsewhere before things got worse."

Due to the way the situation was handled by the president, all five vice-presidents remained and were part of the solution to the firm's problems. Turnover among the work force during this two-year period ran at 14 percent per year—half the rate of the previous two years. Building trust among key stakeholders led to feelings of empowerment. Empowerment led to taking more actions and risks, blaming others less for failures and learning from the mistakes made.

Forming Diagonal-Slice Groups

Another method for empowering others is to involve them directly in the problems to be solved. This is often done through the creation of a *task force*—a group of people given a particular problem to solve or issue to resolve. One type of task force that is particularly stimulating to its members is a *diagonal-slice group.*

A diagonal slice group is an ad hoc group that includes members from different levels of the hierarchy as well as from different functional areas within the venture. In forming such a group, the objective is to include all relevant stakeholders (or representatives of important stakeholder groups) in such a way that no one has his or her immediate boss in the group. By eliminating the boss-subordinate relationship from the group while maintaining involvement of several functions and levels of hierarchy, people feel empowered to speak up and discuss the issues without fear of retribution.

The term diagonal-slice group came to my attention through discussions with Joel DeLuca in 1980. It comes from drawing a diagonal line through a typical organizational chart to identify possible group members.

The benefits of using a diagonal-slice group are its heterogeneity in both level and function with respect to the issues the group is asked to address. The heterogeneous group membership by function leads to many more ideas being considered and different points of view being sought and defended.

The heterogeneity in terms of hierarchy leads to a better understanding of how the ideas suggested are likely to be implemented by people at different levels of the organization. It also permits the ideas of more junior people to be directly heard by senior people who are not their direct superiors.

Diagonal-slice groups, as ad hoc groups, can be convened to address whatever issues the new venture manager chooses. Diagonal-slice groups are most useful when

1. new ideas are needed,
2. buy-in from key stakeholders is essential for an idea to be successfully implemented, and
3. the issue addressed is complex or politically sensitive.

ES&S Advertising. Nancy, the president of the ES&S advertising agency, was able to use a diagonal-slice group to address several questions regarding the agency's possible expansion into international advertising. ES&S has been successful with several medium-to-small clients that market ethnically oriented consumer goods. Annual account billings of $250,000 to $1,500,000 per client are typical. At the end of the fourth year, agency billings exceeded $16,000,000.

While prospecting for new clients, Nancy met people from two different companies who were looking for an agency to handle their products as offered in two or more different cultures (the United States, Puerto Rico and Brazil). ES&S's only office was in Philadelphia—all international activity (which was a minor portion of the business) was handled through international correspondence, travel and client visits. The question Nancy was confronting was whether or not to expand internationally, and if so, what would this mean and how would it be handled?

She formed a diagonal-slice task force to explore the issue. It included her partner, a creative director, an account executive, a writer and a secretary. None of these people had a direct reporting relationship with the others, nor had they worked closely on any particular client's business. Nancy's question to the group was, "What will it take, at all levels and for all functions, to open an office internationally?" Nancy needed their recommendation within two weeks.

While the prospects of opening a second office and soliciting more cross-cultural business looked promising, the group concluded after substantial research, including a survey of other ES&S employees, that the risks outweighed the benefits by a substantial margin. The cost of a second office would be hard to justify with new billings of less than $2,000,000 per office. Only a few existing staff expressed any interest in an international assignment. Expanding internationally would necessitate hiring several people for each international office—people who would not be familiar with the home office. Current ES&S expertise was not in international advertising; ES&S would have to learn as it went along.

The decision not to pursue the international business turned out to be a good one. Within six months, one of the two firms with which Nancy had a discussion was acquired by another firm. ES&S would not have been able to keep the account. Two valued ES&S employees left the firm within the year, placing a notable burden on the remaining staff.

Contrary to these disheartening events, ES&S did well during its fifth year. It was able to expand its business with three of its current clients—increasing billings by 50 percent while costs increased only 32 percent. Nancy was clear that ES&S would not have been able to handle the increased billings without adding substantial staff had she pursued opening an international office.

When asked why she used a diagonal-slice group to assist her in the decision, Nancy said, "If I went with my preference, I would have opened another office. I have great difficulty turning down opportunities—and I personally love international travel. But I knew that it was the agency that would be going international. The agency had to decide. The group I asked to address the issue was a nice mix of people across functions and levels. I figured they would give us an answer that we all could live with. And they did."

Establishing a Collateral Organization

Some of the issues new ventures confront are ongoing, long-term issues. They cannot be solved in a day or week, even by the most capable people. The use of a temporary group to examine these issues is not efficient. Expecting the existing management system to address such issues along with all of their other activities is risky. The urgent issues always drive out any thinking about important but not-yet-urgent issues. An alternative to asking a temporary group to address such issues or relying on the existing management structure, is a *collateral organization.*

A *collateral organization* is a parallel, coexisting group that a new venture manager uses to supplement the existing formal management structure. The primary benefit of using a collateral organization is that it can tailor the standards of behavior, decision-making processes and procedures it uses to the issues at hand, rather than be constrained by the formal organizational systems. (For more information on collateral organizations, see Dale E. Zand, *Information, Organization, and Power: Effective Management in the Knowledge Society* (New York: McGraw Hill, 1981).) Much like a diagonal-slice group, a collateral organization is made up of people who are, or represent, key stakeholders. But this is where the similarity stops.

A collateral organization functions in parallel with the formal hierarchy; it does not replace it. Its members are often drawn from the upper echelons of the venture rather than from all levels of the organization. This parallel organization is empowered to address select issues in whatever ways it views as appropriate—independent of the way other decisions are made within the venture.

Collateral organizations are distinct from the formal organization in several ways.

- Their purpose is to identify and attend to issues not resolved by the formal, primary organization.
- Their formation permits new combinations of people, new channels of communication and new ways of viewing situations.
- The new venture manager chooses which system to use for each major issue confronting the venture—the formal organization or the collateral organization.
- The outputs of the collateral organization are inputs to the formal system.
- The collateral organization operates with its own set of norms.

Collateral organizations empower their members to take on the venture's challenges as if they were its only leadership. They can collect information, conduct analyses and discuss issues as they see appropriate. Once their analysis leads to suggestions and recommendations that are acceptable to the group, the group presents them to the management of the formal organization. It is then up to the formal organization to decide how to proceed.

MCG's Leadership Transition.   The Management Consulting Group (MCG) had been in existence for about seven years. Growth was rapid during the early years, as each new professional added brought in some new business. It seemed that every major corporation in America was hiring consultants, and MCG was getting its share of the opportunities.

A founder (and MCG's first CEO) became sick and was eventually diagnosed as having cancer. It was not clear how long he would continue functioning as the head of MCG—his health was clearly deteriorating, but no one wanted to confront him directly about his duties. It was impossible to determine whether he would recover or become worse. One thing was clear: He did not want to give up his role as CEO.

With some encouragement from several of the other founders and senior partners, the CEO decided to form a collateral organization to address key issues facing the company, including a CEO succession plan. Rather than use the formal organization, a collateral organization was formed to do the following:

- Involve a wider group of people in the process—particularly at the middle level of the organization
- Reduce the likelihood of conflict among senior partners who might want the CEO position
- Maintain business as usual with respect to MCG's clients through the formal organization

The collateral organization began meeting weekly, raising and discussing a variety of issues the formal organization agreed should be dealt with through this parallel structure. It was proposed that a CEO-elect be identified to assume the leadership of MCG in 18 months if the current CEO's health permitted his continuing on as head for that long. Through a series of meetings, followed by reporting-out sessions to all of the partners, a process was agreed to for identifying the CEO-elect.

The partners interested in the CEO role identified themselves. Each prepared a brief oral statement of his or her views on key issues and intended approach to the job. A vote was taken that included all full-time professional staff as to their preference for the new CEO. The result of this vote was reviewed by the collateral organization, and a CEO-elect was identified by the collateral organization members. This was the first time in anyone's memory that such a process was used to identify a new CEO of a consulting firm.

Three months after this vote, the CEO-elect assumed the CEO role due to the failing health of the previous CEO. The transition was smooth and without problem. The new CEO has the active support of the partners and professional staff. As one of the contenders for the CEO role states, "The process we used to identify Jack's successor was different than anyone expected. By empowering a group of more junior professionals to address the issue off-line, we were able to continue serving our clients without the internal political stuff getting in the way. We are all pleased with the performance of our new CEO—this has been the easiest transition of leadership I have witnessed."

Using Self-Directed Teams (SDTs)

A *self-directed team* is a group of individuals collectively responsible for accomplishing specific tasks *and* learning from their joint activities. This concept goes by many names: self-directed work teams, self-managing teams, relationship management groups and high-involvement work groups, among others. The teams themselves vary based on what makes sense for the venture.

In general, an SDT is a group of employees (anywhere from 4 to 15) who are responsible for a product or process. The team plans the work and performs it. Many new ventures begin with but one SDT—the entire venture. Over time, as employees are hired, as middle management is created and as standard procedures replace informal ones, the initial SDT is consumed by traditional management structures. Whether or not the traditional management structures should be the backbone of the new venture is an issue that needs to be addressed by the venture's management.

SDTs differ from other types of organizing frameworks in several ways.

- SDTs emphasize self-management within a flat organizational hierarchy.

- Responsibility for pursuing the venture's mission and vision—and accomplishing its objectives—is assumed by SDT members who are expected to develop a comprehensive skill base germane to the work to be done.

- Information among SDT members is openly shared and used to solve immediate problems as well as develop longer-term goals and objectives.

- SDTs are often responsible for developing the venture's strategy with respect to the product or service for which they are responsible.

Within a manufacturing organization, an SDT might be the primary production unit—including engineering, production, quality control and shipping responsibilities. In a service organization, an SDT might have full client responsibility—addressing all of the clients' needs. SDTs are typically accountable for production or service delivery, quality, costs and schedules.

Some SDTs have responsibility for interviewing and hiring new people, doing performance appraisals, making repairs, monitoring statistical process control and coordinating activities with other areas. Members, with the help of training, develop a variety of technical skills to make the unit autonomous as well as the interpersonal skills needed to function effectively as a team.

SDTs empower their members to run a portion of the venture—not just a function or part of a function. The success of SDTs in work organizations is attributed to this empowerment. The new venture manager's challenge is to determine, with the aid of the work force, what the logical team unit is as the venture continues to grow. If SDTs can be created and employed to address specific parts of the venture, the new venture manager's role shifts toward the leadership role, allowing the SDTs to handle the management role.

MEDC's New Venture Challenge. The Management Educational Development Center (MEDC) of a consumer goods organization had been developing courses for internal use for nearly six years. After careful design and piloting, each course was made available to all of the human resource units within the firm. With over 14,000 management employees, the parent organization felt that their corporate investment in management education was worth the expense.

With a change in management and a serious downturn in profits, the parent organization decided to cut funding to MEDC—if it was to survive, it would have to be a profit center. They wanted MEDC to actively market its programs, not only within the organization but to others. MEDC was to be viewed as an independent profit center, with all of the challenges associated with sustaining and growing a business poststart-up.

MEDC houses about 30 professionals and uses an additional 20 consultants in its ongoing activities. They were organized as a single unit, with several separate functions, including program managers, program developers, conference coordinators, computer support, materials production, distribution and graphic arts. There was no marketing role, as all previous programs had been conducted in-house.

As the head of the unit, Chris decided to approach the new challenge through SDTs organized around their individual curriculums: financial management and control, marketing, business strategy, managing people and information systems. Each of these areas has two or three courses that are offered internally, two to five times each year.

The SDT structure places complete control and responsibility on each of five work teams. Each is responsible for its own bottom line. The work teams control their pricing, instructors, class size, frequency of offering and the like. They are also responsible for all selling activities outside of the company, including prospecting new clients, developing a client relationship, delivering the programs and evaluation/feedback of program performance. MEDC handles internal marketing issues and coordinates a single marketing brochure for the entire unit. Each SDT produces its own brochures for the specific courses offered.

During its first year of operation as a profit center, MEDC is doing well. The SDTs act as autonomous units, seeking clients where the interest is most strong. Information regarding the SDTs' selling activity is shared at monthly meetings, thereby providing an opportunity to jointly sell a prospective client that is of interest to more than one unit.

The Marketing SDT is doing the best. It has been able to leverage the parent company's reputation as an excellent marketer. It has 14 programs scheduled across six different clients for the next quarter. Based on a price of $124 per person per day of training, they expect revenues of $156,000 next quarter. Costs are projected at $68,000.

By empowering the members of each SDT to sell, design and deliver, MEDC functions as a composite of five education centers rather than one. Chris describes it this way: "Our old structure worked fine when we had corporate funding. Our focus was on developing quality education for practicing managers. We didn't have to consider marketing or controlling costs or generating revenues.

"That has all changed. Our new structure links to the changes that have taken place. We still do development but not as much as before. We look for a client that wants something new; then we develop it for them—at a price. Selling and delivery are the real challenges today. We are doing well in Marketing; we hope to be able to learn from their efforts to improve our success in the other four areas as well."

ARE PEOPLE FEELING EMPOWERED?

It is not enough to say or believe that others within your venture are empowered to take actions to keep the venture growing profitably. Many new venture managers believe that their people are empowered, but their people do not express the same belief. The venture manager says, "Of course people have the power to call on a new client, negotiate a better deal with a distributor, respond to an irate customer or sign for a large order." And the people say, "Sure, we can call on a new client alone—if we get approval first and the boss doesn't have the time to come along" or "Negotiating a deal with a distributor means changing delivery terms; we would never be permitted to make big concessions to get more sales."

There are many more examples. I have heard hundreds of reasons why the people whom the venture manager believes are empowered do not feel empowered. Most of the reasons are associated with the issue of *control*. People do not believe that they have the right to control the venture's position or posturing within a situation. When new venture managers are confronted with this information, they typically admit that they do want to be "kept informed"—which translates into "ask me before you act" in the minds of many employees.

To empower people, the venture's direction (mission, vision and objectives) and culture must provide the initial empowerment. "Kept informed" must come to mean "Let me know in a timely manner how things are going."

Through building trust, forming task forces, creating a collateral organization and using self-directed teams, new venture managers are taking concrete actions that transfer the control of a situation or issue to others. This is the way people begin to feel empowered. The venture's direction provides the framework, the culture provides a supportive process and the management techniques provide the specific and tangible permission to take charge.

Consider the following questions as you examine the extent to which your key people really feel empowered to move your venture forward:

• If you went on a two-week business trip without advance notice to the staff, who would do what while you were away?

- What would not get done that would have been done if you were present?

- How often do people ask for permission or approval?

- List each of your direct reports separately.

- Keep a tally of the number of times each direct report asks for permission, asks for approval or provides after-the-fact updates on events over a two-day period.

- Who do you trust with key clients?

- Who do you trust with the venture's capital and finances?

- Who do you trust to handle key personnel issues (hiring, salary changes, firings)?

- How may committees, task forces, diagonal-slice groups or other ad hoc groups exist within the venture today?

- What is each group charged to do? What is their deliverable? When is it needed?

- Are there discrete parts or units of the business that could be organized as SDTs?

- Are they functioning as SDTs?

- What needs to change before you can empower them to run their own business?

- Are people learning from what they are doing? Really?

- What is it that people are learning?

It is these last two questions that lead to the final chapter, which concerns creating a learning venture. Without ongoing learning, the venture will prematurely plateau well short of its potential. When people navigate in uncharted waters, they need to plot their courses as they go, updating it at each turn as new information becomes available. They need to be learning through their thoughts, feelings and actions. They need to be capturing this knowledge within themselves and sharing it with their key stakeholders. To do this, they create a learning venture.

10

■─────────────────■

Sustaining Rapid Growth—Creating a *Learning* Venture

This book has been about how ventures learn and then use what they have learned to prosper. How a venture learns, apart from the learning of its individual members, is not fully understood—nor is what is understood easy to convey. Of those who have tried to communicate the principles of a learning organization, Peter Senge's work is outstanding. In his book, *The Fifth Discipline: The Art & Practice of the Learning Organization* (Doubleday, 1990), Senge discusses five disciplines that people must master to create a learning organization. The disciplines require organizational members to do the following:

- Understand, articulate and at times change their *mental models* of how things work
- Build a *shared vision* of the future
- Develop *personal mastery*
- Facilitate and generate *team learning*
- Apply *systems thinking* to issues, problems and opportunities that the venture experiences

In Senge's terms, a discipline is a developmental path for acquiring a particular set of skills and competencies. Some people have a substantial amount of these skills and competencies already (either developed or through an innate gift); others work to develop proficiency in these skills and competencies through practice, feedback and more practice.

Each part of this book has focused on developing one of these five disciplines in new venture managers. To see what we have accomplished, we need to visit these disciplines in light of the challenges of growing a new venture profitably.

UNDERSTANDING, ARTICULATING AND CHANGING MENTAL MODELS

A *mental model* is a set of beliefs about how a system works. We all have thousands of mental models in our minds, most of which are labeled and stored for future use. Each model was created when we learned something new or experienced something different in what we thought we knew.

Our mental models are like recorded tapes that we store in our brains to be recalled and played in the future. Several mental models associated with growing a new venture profitably are developed and shared in the first four chapters of this book. These models were derived from discussions with hundreds of managers confronting the rapid-growth stage of their ventures over 20 years. They have withstood both tests of time and context.

The most general model is the 4-Box Model. This model identifies the key variables associated with strategic planning and implementation. As suggested by the arrows between each of the four boxes, the venture's strategy involves relationships among the external environment, internal environment, possible alternatives and intended actions.

Mental models, such as the 4-Box Model, contain ingrained assumptions and generalizations that reflect how we see both the world and a new venture as functioning. Mental models have two components: (1) the variables of the model (such as the bullet points in the 4-Box Model) and (2) the relationships among the variables (such as decreasing price to stimulate sales). Both the variables and their interrelationships must be known and understood if you are to use the mental model to guide the venture's decisions and actions.

The 4-Box Model contains many variables and relationships with which many new venture managers are familiar. If it did not, it would not be a useful mental model. The 4-Box Model articulates the mental models of hundreds of new venture managers in sufficient detail for others to test their understanding of the model's variables and the interrelationships among these variables in their business situations. Venture success is associated with building an accurate and useful mental model that reflects the dynamics of the business—overlooking any of the key variables or relationships that actually exist in the business can be fatal. By articulating these variables and suggesting their most common relationships, the 4-Box Model helps to reduce this risk.

Unfortunately, the detail of the 4-Box Model makes it hard to apply it in its entirety in an ongoing manner. Our mental capacity can only handle so much—and the 4-Box Model is too much. To overcome this problem, the model is discussed as an analytical model to *facilitate strategic thinking*. It can be used in its entirety from time to time when one is doing annual planning or longer-term thinking. For day-to-day activity, simpler mental models are needed.

What are these more parsimonious mental models? Here is a brief version of the mental models contained in the 4-Box Model that are discussed in Part I.

- *Consumer needs.* Identify what consumers *want* and give it to them. Identify what they don't want and don't give it to them.

- *Competitors' strengths and weaknesses.* Examine the competition. Avoid challenging their strengths. Focus the venture's efforts on areas where competitors are weak and unlikely to retaliate.

- *Trends that could affect the business.* Identify relevant trends. Ride trends, don't fight them.

- *Business profit and loss dynamics.* Know how you make money in your business better than anyone else and never forget it when making business decisions. Share how you make money widely within the venture. You cannot expect others to help you make money if they do not understand how their behaviors affect the bottom line.

- *Financial, marketing and behavioral goals.* Know what you want, in painstaking detail, all the way down to each customer and employee behavior that must be influenced to accomplish each goal.

- *Strengths, problems, opportunities and threats (SPOT).* Know your business situation—leverage its strengths, solve or work around its problems, take opportunities that leverage its strengths and/or solve its problems while minimizing future threats, and protect against all high-cost threats materializing early. Use your SPOT analysis to answer the question What can we do?

- *Competitive advantage.* Know it, share it widely within the venture and ensure that every action taken reinforces, leverages or builds on it. Your competitive advantage should answer the question Why should they buy it from us? (from their point of view).

- *Target markets.* Less is more—the essence of your venture's strategy is denial. Focus on the most viable prospects that you can reach with a message that they want to hear.

- *Positioning.* Capture a distinctive piece of the consumer's mind for your products and services. Claim it, develop it, own it. Whenever a potential customer thinks of your venture's product category, he or she should have an image in his or her mind that is your product.

- *Product, price, place and promotions (the four P's).* These are the tactics of marketing—they work together to create your offering. Think of them as four peas in a pod. They are all part of the same system. Sell *product* benefits, not features. *Price* for growth with profits, leaving no money on the table. *Distribute* through channels that your target consumers want to use. *Promote* for high-impact, short-term sales increases.

- *Communications mix.* Identify the many *theys* that need to know about the venture's products, services, values, activities and culture. Tell them what they are interested in hearing—promptly and ethically.

- *Product programs.* Focus on the design and execution of high-quality programs, targeted to the venture's primary target groups, then deliver them flawlessly.

- *Monitoring and research systems.* Monitor and measure those things that link directly to the actions and activities that answer the question How do we make money in this business? If you are not open to the idea of doing something differently as a result of the research data collected, don't bother collecting it. Match the cost of collecting information with the risk being reduced by its use.

If growing a new venture profitably only required analysis and strategic thinking, the 4-Box Model and its corollary mental models would be all that are needed. As new venture managers know, there is more to what they do than analysis and thinking.

We continued the development of mental models in Part II. The first mental model presented in Part II was in Chapter 5, "Direction, Direction, Direction." Contrary to most of the new business venture literature that treats direction as a singular concept, we view it as having three distinct elements.

1. *Direction as destination*—sharing the venture's mission, vision and objectives

2. *Direction as heading and course*—identifying and following the venture's distinctive competence

3. *Direction through management style*—creating a shared sense of values and an organizational culture that supports rapid, profitable growth

These three elements of direction reflect a mental model that has emerged over two decades of working with people trying to grow a business profitably. What their subordinates and key stakeholders continually look for is direction in one or more of these ways. Sharing the venture's direction in some of these ways but not in others is insufficient to energize all of the key stakeholders much of the time. If the venture cannot give the stakeholders what they want, they will go elsewhere.

The next mental model developed is a stakeholder grid, as shown in Figure 6.1 (page 130). While new venture managers know much about some of their stakeholders (particularly those who are most vocal), they often fail to consider the array of stakeholders that affect their business. The stakeholder categories are used to expand your mental model of "who has a stake in this venture."

A natural tendency of many new venture managers is to narrow their view of stakeholders, rather than expand it. It is not easy to think of others as having an important stake in what you have created. Accepting a model that begins to sound like "what is mine is yours, and what is yours is yours" is uncomfortable.

To shift from a mental model that identifies only a few stakeholders to one that is comprehensive takes energy, which is not always available during the day-to-day activities of a venture. Yet this energy must be found if the many diverse stakeholders are to be satisfied. It will be the one stakeholder that you did not satisfy who harms the venture—be it an angry customer, a put-off business analyst or a left-out supplier.

One way to make this effort easier is to focus on the specific wants that each stakeholder group has for your venture. Customers, shareholders, employees, suppliers and other stakeholders all desire some of their wants to be satisfied by the venture—but not all of their wants. Get to know the stakeholders and focus on giving them what they want from you that you are prepared to give.

We introduced the W-cubed model as a way of thinking about what it is that the many stakeholders want that links to what the venture can do. As the model shown in Figure 7.2 (page 164) suggests, simultaneously satisfying these three questions leads to venture success:

1. What does the venture want?

2. What do the key stakeholders want?

3. What can the venture do?

Find answers to these questions that are mutually satisfactory. The answers will lead to the greatest venture success and the least stakeholder resistance.

New venture managers report that W-cubed is one of the most useful mental models they have. It is easy to remember, it can be applied while on the job and it yields useful insights into what the barriers are to proposed actions. As a heuristic, W-cubed permits discovery through its use—a key aspect of a learning organization.

Several other mental models have been shared as part of the dialogue on obtaining rapid and profitable growth. Models about learning, leading and managing are part of chapter 8. Chapter 9 focuses on models for creating a culture, working in groups and empowering others.

Each of the mental models proposed has been observed to reflect the ways successful new venture managers think and act as they seek the sweet spot. To the extent that these models have worked for others, they can be made to work for you.

BUILD A SHARED VISION OF THE FUTURE

A second learning discipline is the ability to build a shared vision. This requires the skills of creating, unearthing or otherwise forming a shared picture of the future. We explored this idea in chapter 5 as the first of the three elements of direction. It is so essential to the success of a venture that it is worth revisiting—with the goal of refining the venture's mission and vision to be more inspiring than before.

- *What is the venture's mission? Its reason for being?* Without looking back to chapter 5, can you state your answers in ten words or less?

- *What is your vision for the new venture? What is the inspiration the venture provides others for their efforts?* Describe it in at least 50 words, symbols and/or pictures.

Now that the vision has been created, how will you share it? Circulating a mission and vision statement is a start. But how inspired have you become reading someone else's vision? Telling people about your vision is a stronger approach. We are sometimes inspired by what we hear, but not often.

You must find ways to get people involved with the vision—they need to see it for themselves, to feel it and to talk about it. The goal is for them to own the vision as much as you do. Without this level of sharing, the vision will not provide the depth of inspiration and direction that you desire.

DEVELOP PERSONAL MASTERY

A new venture can only learn to the extent that its members can learn. We know that people learn best when they have a personal sense of direction (mission, vision and objectives) and their efforts are supported by people and institutions they value. Learning occurs through feedback that is heard and accepted as part of the skill-development process. Both positive and negative feedback lead to learning when the environment supports individual development as well as venture success.

The skill areas and personal competencies that lead to personal mastery are discussed in chapter 8. Not only must people learn how to learn through tapping into their natural discovery processes, they must be able to balance the skills of a manager with the skills of a leader. While these skills are not incompatible, they are seldom naturally exhibited by the same people.

People have predispositions to lead or to manage. New venture managers tend to exhibit stronger leadership skills. This is why many institutions replace new venture managers with others once a venture has been successfully established. Too much leadership without adequate controls leads to high costs and little profits. Overmanaging or overleading results in venture stagnation—the former through overcontrol, the latter through too much opportunity seeking.

FACILITATE AND GENERATE TEAM LEARNING

The fourth discipline is *team learning*—the ability of a group of people to add value to each other and the group so as to overcome the tendency of performing only as effectively as the average person in the group, or worse yet, the least competent person in the group.

Chapter 9 focuses on team learning through empowering others. This can occur through creating a culture that facilitates dialogue and shared understandings of how things are done in the venture. Building trust among venture members furthers team learning through the interpersonal bonds that are created as a result of each trust episode. Working in ad hoc groups, such as diagonal-slice groups and collateral organizations, permits people to suspend their typical operating assumptions and enter into a genuine bond of thinking together.

Self-directed teams empower their members to manage the production of a product or process. Since SDTs are typically organized around the primary tasks to be accomplished within the venture that relate to growth and profits, they are a particularly relevant forum for team learning.

Yet, neither the venture's culture nor management techniques for empowering people assure team learning. Team learning is more than the culture or an activity. It is the alignment of individual, specialized skills and wills such that the group and the individuals are one. We have all had such experiences—the feeling is almost magical. We have also seen it in others, most commonly in sports teams that really come together to do the unbelievable. While it may not be easy to describe or to create team learning, it is what is to be sought in each of the venture's small group activities.

APPLY SYSTEMS THINKING TO ISSUES, PROBLEMS AND OPPORTUNITIES THAT THE VENTURE EXPERIENCES

Systems thinking is what Peter Senge proposes as the *fifth discipline*. This skill must use and go beyond the mastery of the other disciplines for ventures to learn from their members, their history and their ongoing activities.

While we have attempted to create a system of ideas to explore during the rapid-growth phase of a new venture, it is up to the new venture managers to incorporate these ideas into their system. A few additional ideas may help this to occur—for example, watching out for and avoiding the "gotcha's" and looking for the system dynamics within the system.

Avoiding the Gotcha's

When you fall into an antiquated way of thinking or into a pattern of beliefs from the past that no longer apply, you have been "got." Be on the lookout for the following five gotcha's. Each gotcha will contribute to decisions that undermine the effectiveness of the system being built.

1. *The new venture manager and new venture growth and profits are tightly linked—Gotcha!* This gotcha is a natural outgrowth of the past success of the venture. New venture managers are so instrumental in the venture's success that it is easy to believe that they *are* the venture. An air of self-righteousness and omnipotence surrounds them—sometimes of their own doing, but equally often from an admiring staff.

The new venture is no more the new venture manager than is any person in the manager's position. We assume and accept positions in life because we believe we can add and receive value through performing the duties of that position. When we slip into thinking that we are the position—that the venture is the manager—we lose perspective. We also become less subject to the interpersonal influences and subtle business cues around us that have led to the venture's success.

One way to avoid this gotcha is to have at least two replacements for yourself in mind. Who will assume leadership when you are no longer the new venture manager?

2. *Something is screwed up. Who is to blame? Gotcha!* Things occur differently than planned. When this leads to a gap between where we thought we would be and where we are, we call it a problem. When things go wrong, when there is a problem, there is an ever-present tendency to find out who or what is to blame. If we find the blame, we can correct the problem or at least prevent it from happening again. This is the logic behind our search for the culprit.

Rarely is there just one cause to any problem. Why blame the person who was most directly involved with the problem? Why not blame his or her supervisor? The supervisor should have trained the person better, monitored the person's behavior more closely or hired a different person entirely. Or let's blame the subordinate—that person had greater technical knowledge, so he or she should have helped prevent the problem.

When our thinking is dominated by "should have's" and "who did it's," we've been "got" again. Most undesired events have many causes—some quite immediate, many more embedded in past decisions and actions. *Blame is a lousy emotion; it debilitates those blamed and leads to feelings of guilt in the ones doing the blaming.*

3. *More is better—Gotcha!* As Jack Cohen, an applied statistics professor at New York University, says about conducting many statistical analyses to find what you hope to find, *more is not better; better is better.*

We frequently fall into the more-is-better trap. We place an order for more supplies. The order is late. We call to check on the order but are not satisfied with the answer. Then we place a duplicate order with another supplier. More is better.

If we continue in this way of thinking, we overextend our financial resources to cover our excess supply. Then we do it again—we seek more financial backing. More is better. Stop the cycle. During periods of rapid growth, you can do more with less more often than you can do more with more. People like challenges more than they like stocking inventory or paying back bank loans. More importantly, excess resources makes for careless thinking. Wasted time, wasted resources, wasted energy. *Make less more.*

4. *Focusing on events as key indicators of cause and effect—Gotcha!* We are a culture focused on events. Just listen to the financial reports on any day, on any channel. The stock market went up (or down) because of one or more events that also occurred that day. The humor in such reports is that it is a different event every day that has caused the stock price movement. It is as if every investor has a predetermined set of events that he or she expects to occur in order to make buy-sell decisions. The financial markets are much too complex for any small set of events to make any difference. Yet, we like to keep our world view simple: Interest rates go up, the market goes down.

Events occur. The cause-effect chain among the events that are key to a venture's success are neither simple nor constant. Avoid focusing on events; *focus on the pattern and flow of events that generate revenues and costs for the business.* Focus on the trends that affect consumer wants and competitors' offerings. Focus on the flow of people, money and energy through the venture—this is where the cause-effect links are to be found.

5. *Following incremental changes to places you do* not *want to visit—Gotcha!* Have you ever found yourself in one place when you really wanted to be in another? Incrementalism may have "gotcha" there. We often make small changes in what we do—the manufacturing process, our selling activities, altered product features—in an effort to improve things. Sometimes the improvements lead to other improvements.

Before long, we have a different product, a different competitive advantage or a different supplier. Is this what we wanted? Is it what is wanted now in light of our mission, vision and objectives? If not, it is time to either redirect our efforts to get to where we wanted to be or change our mission, vision and objectives.

Incremental changes are a way of life. Without a clear sense of direction, we can increment our way to Chicago when we really wanted to go to St. Louis. The parable of the boiled frog captures this gotcha quite well. If you raise the temperature of the water in which a frog sits one degree each five minutes, you will be able to boil the frog. Each increment is too small for the frog to notice; the end result is not what the frog wanted, but each degree of warmth was acceptable. Incremental changes keep things moving; put the periscope up every day or two to see if your venture is still on course.

Toward Systems Thinking—Finding the System Dynamics

A second way to develop the discipline of systems thinking is to look for the dynamics within the systems that we inhabit. How does the system really work? We have asked this question in many ways throughout each chapter.

• How do you make money in this business?

• What behaviors do you need to influence to achieve your objectives?

• What are the points of contact with each consumer that are subject to influence?

• Who are the venture's key stakeholders, and what do they want?

As you answer these questions, you are employing your mental models and are implicitly stating the variables and relationships you see within the venture's system. As you explore the dynamics of your system, keep the following ideas in mind.

1. *Look for today's problems in yesterday's solutions.* Systems involve elements that are connected both in space (context) and time. Yesterday's solutions are connected to today's events. Some of yesterday's solutions probably have effects that were not expected. What might they be? As you look for and attempt to solve today's problems, seek out their causes in yesterday's solutions.

2. *Cause and effect may* not *be closely related in time or context.* We give someone a salary raise and we expect to see them working harder the next day. We send someone to a training session and we expect to see results within a couple of weeks. We develop a target marketing grid, select the prime prospects and start a major selling effort, but sales do not increase as expected that quarter.

Rarely are cause and effect closely related in time within new business ventures. The newness of our activities implies the need for others to change from what they were doing to what we would like them to do. Change takes time, just as creating our vision for the venture takes time. Having articulated a vision is different than having people be inspired by that vision.

People need time to grow and develop ownership of new ideas. If we expect immediate or even quick results, we fall prey to the gotcha's: We assume more is better, and we focus on events as key indicators of cause and effect. Neither is true.

3. *Every action has an equal and opposite reaction.* This basic law of physics applies to all systems—business ventures as well as mechanical equipment. Yet, we forget this principle when we take actions. We solve a problem, satisfy a customer or praise an employee; then something else goes wrong.

Systems push back. Doing something for one part of a system will often result in some other part of the system behaving differently. We do not always see the system's reaction to our actions because we are not looking in the right places. For example, we alter our product price. Competitors are part of the system, so they react to our actions. Customers are part of the system, so they react to our actions. A stakeholder analysis helps to identify the many players in a system. When we satisfy (or anger) one stakeholder, we have an effect on some of the other stakeholders. Every action has a reaction—we need to get better at predicting the reactions, scanning for them and then building the likely reaction into our strategy.

4. *There is no one and nothing to blame.* With a system dynamics view of the venture, the venture's system encompasses all of its stakeholders. There is no one out there to blame for the venture's problems because "out there" becomes "in here" within an enlarged stakeholder analysis. Blaming others, as this gotcha suggests, does not get at the causes of problems. Looking for others to blame consumes valuable time. Once a person is blamed, he or she defends, withdraws and becomes alienated. This is not what we want. There is no blame worth this cost. So why blame?

One of the risks in writing a book on new venture growth is that readers will attempt to model their ventures on the experiences of others. Nothing could be further from our purpose. For this reason we have kept many of the examples short, and for the longer examples we have used disguised names or provided only a part of the venture's business situation.

The model you must keep in mind is the systems view that relates to your business—how your business makes money, what your constituencies want and what values and culture you want to create for your employees. Each chapter in this book has been written to provide you with a set of disciplines to develop in your quest for growth and profits. These chapters can provide you with a host of areas and ideas to think about; they should not tell you what to think.

Index

■————————————————————■

.